Received on Nov

" " Kathy 70th BD

AUNTY ACID'S
GETTING OLDER
CREATED BY GED BACKLAND

GIBBS SMITH
TO ENRICH AND INSPIRE HUMANKIND

HELLO, FOLKS, WELCOME TO MY LITTLE BOOK ON GETTING OLDER

I've had a lifetime of laughs, loves, good times, bad times and too many bottles of vino to keep count... But all that enjoyment has taken its toll on this temple I call me. Hell, I think of running away more now as an adult than I did when I was a kid!

Youth huh! It's freakin' wasted on the young.

So read on and enjoy Aunty Acid's pages filled with the perils of sagging boobs, instructions on how to grow old disgracefully and where to find, and dive head first, into that elusive fountain of youth!

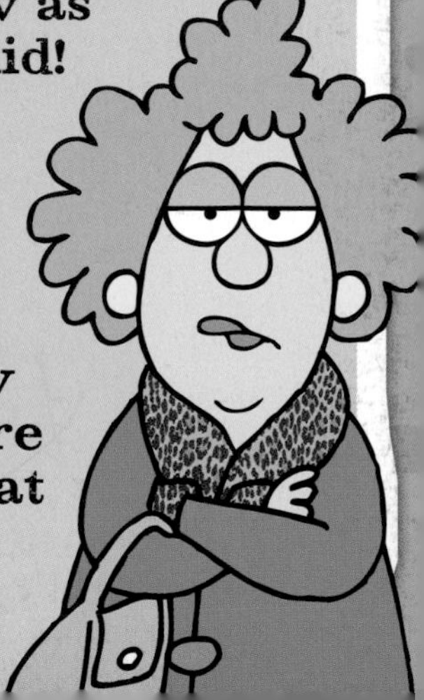

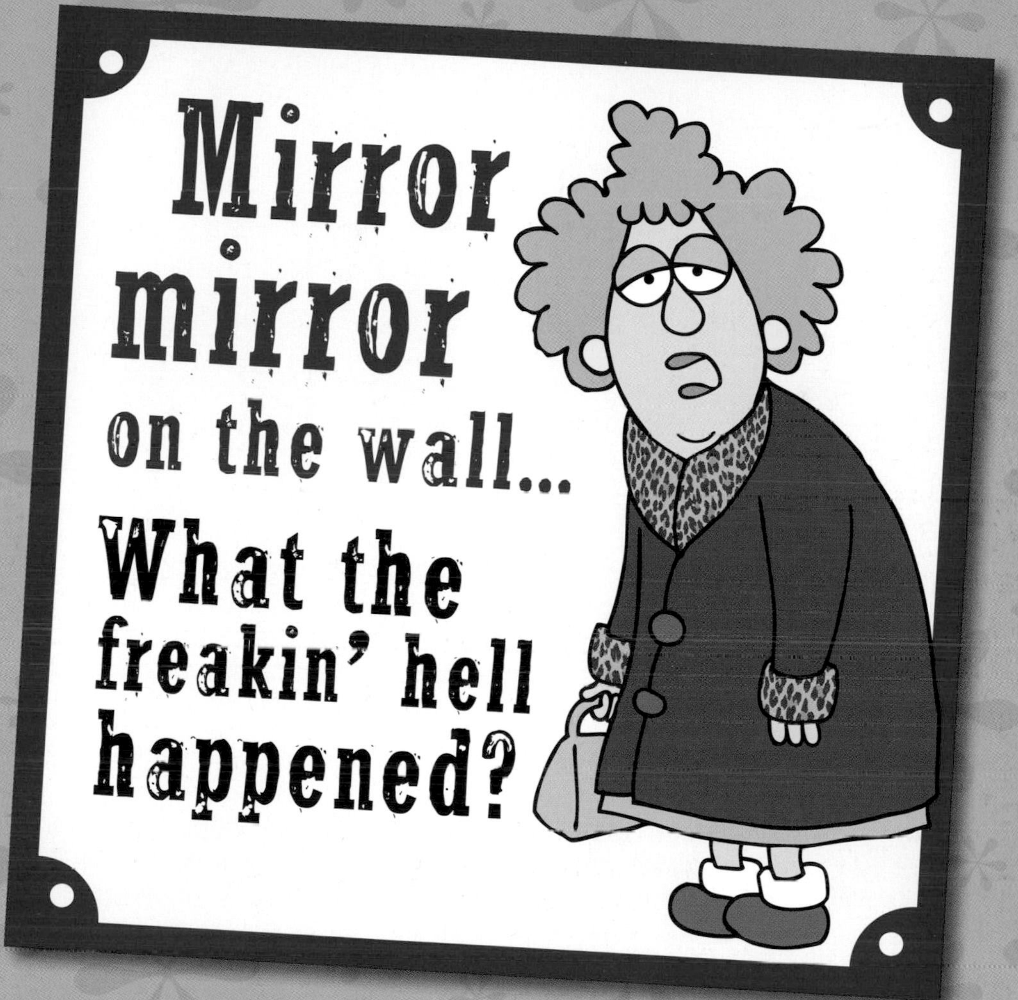
Mirror
mirror
on the wall...
What the
freakin' hell
happened?

My doctor told me to avoid any unnecessary stress.

So I didn't open his bill.

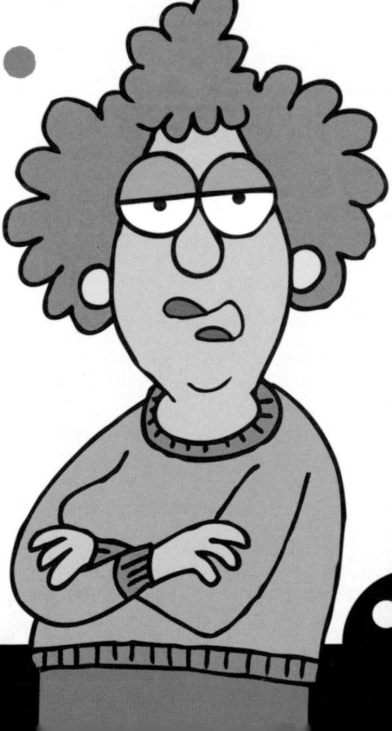

Be nice to

nurses.

They keep doctors from killing you.

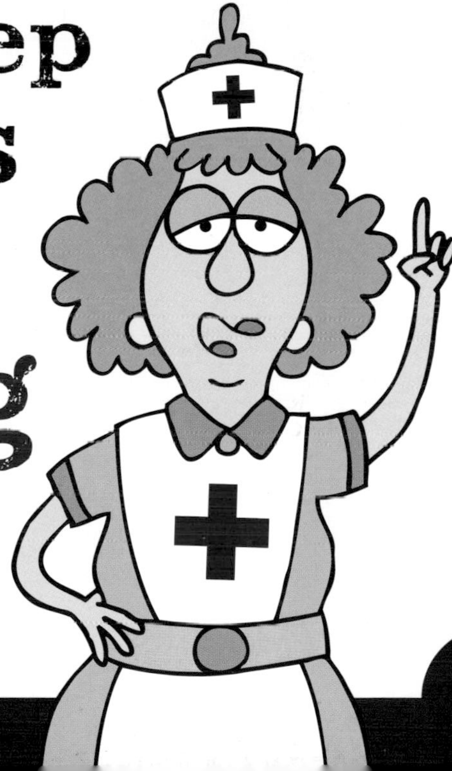

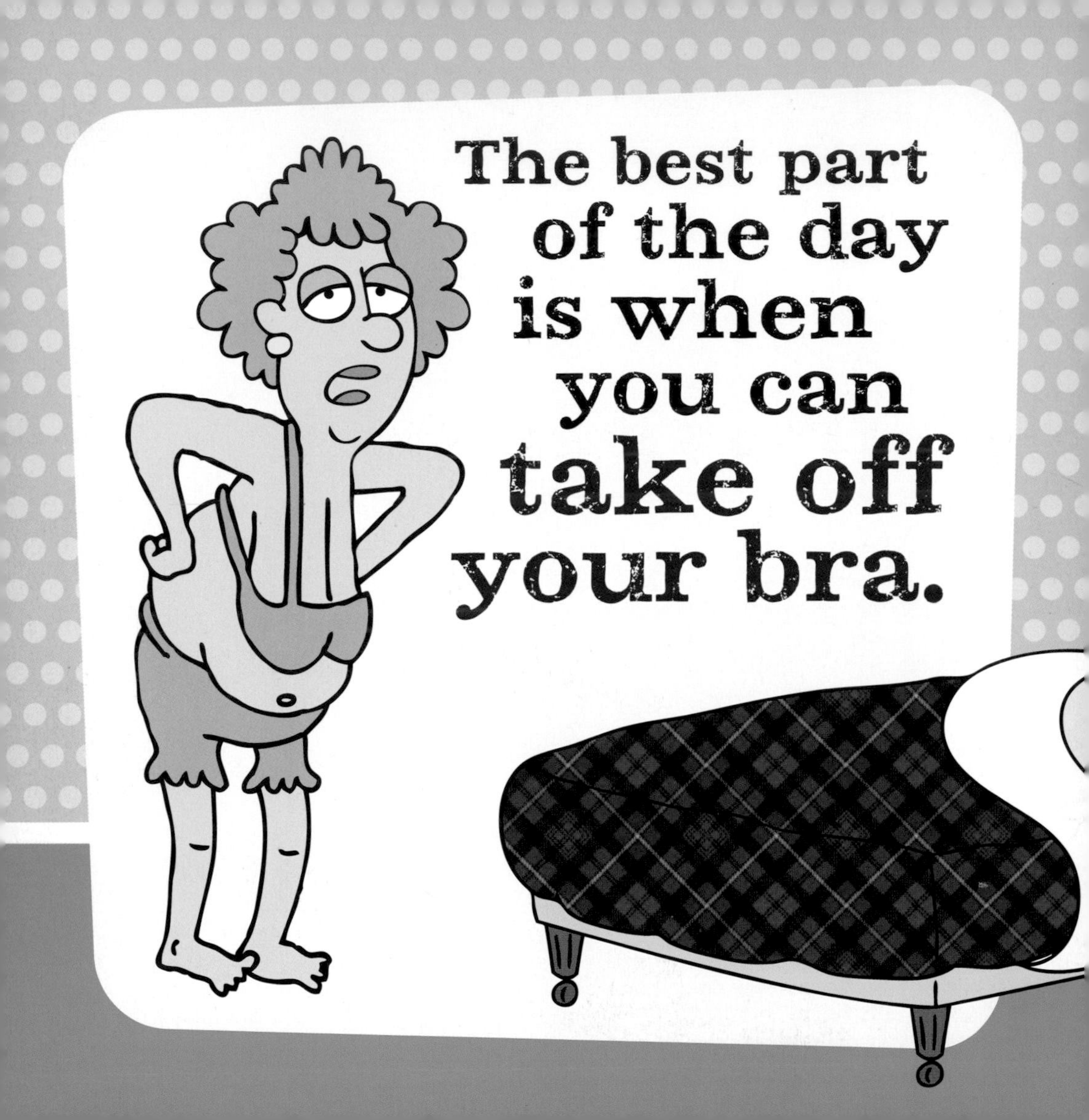
The best part
of the day
is when
you can
take off
your bra.

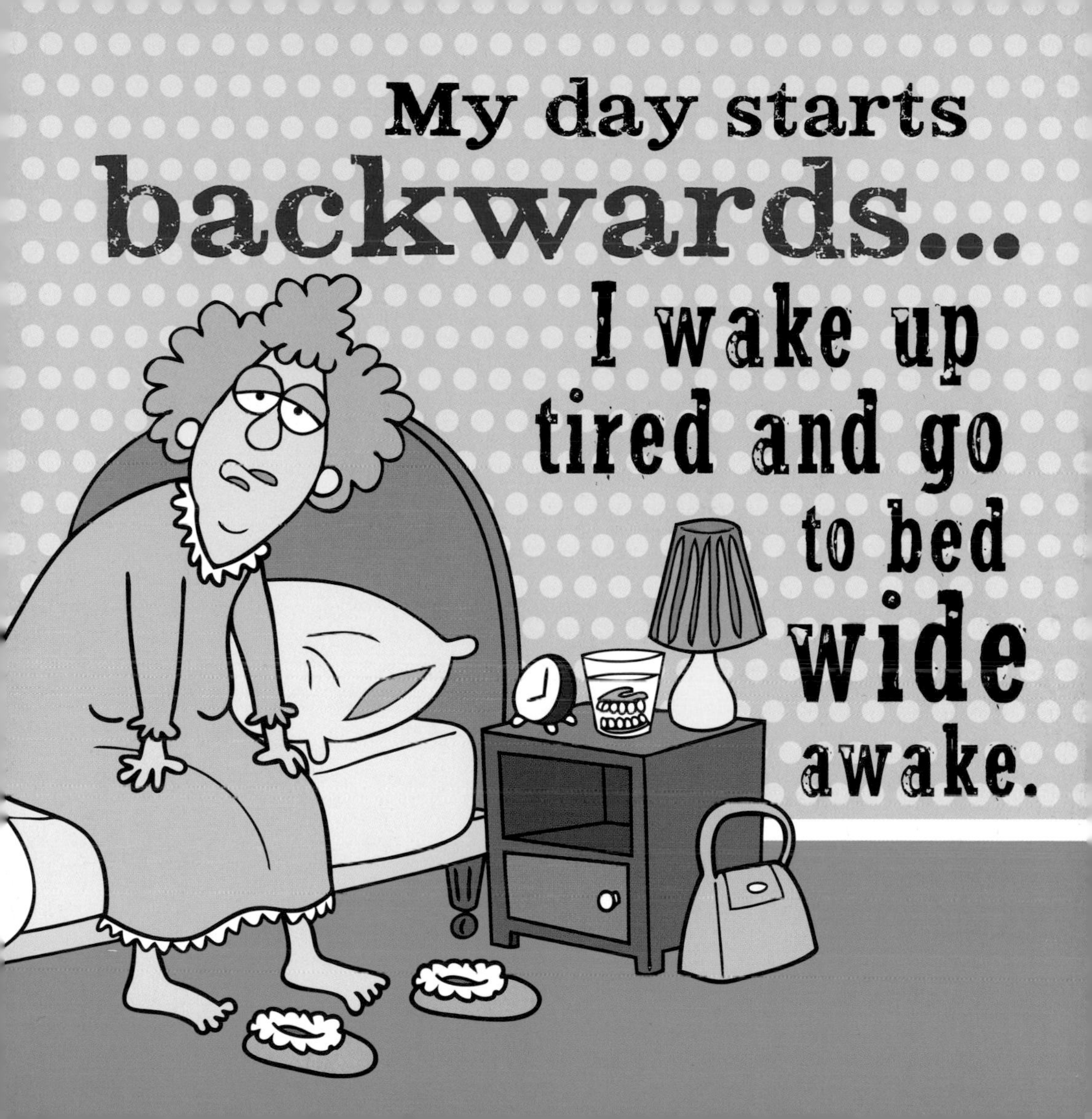
My day starts backwards...
I wake up tired and go to bed wide awake.

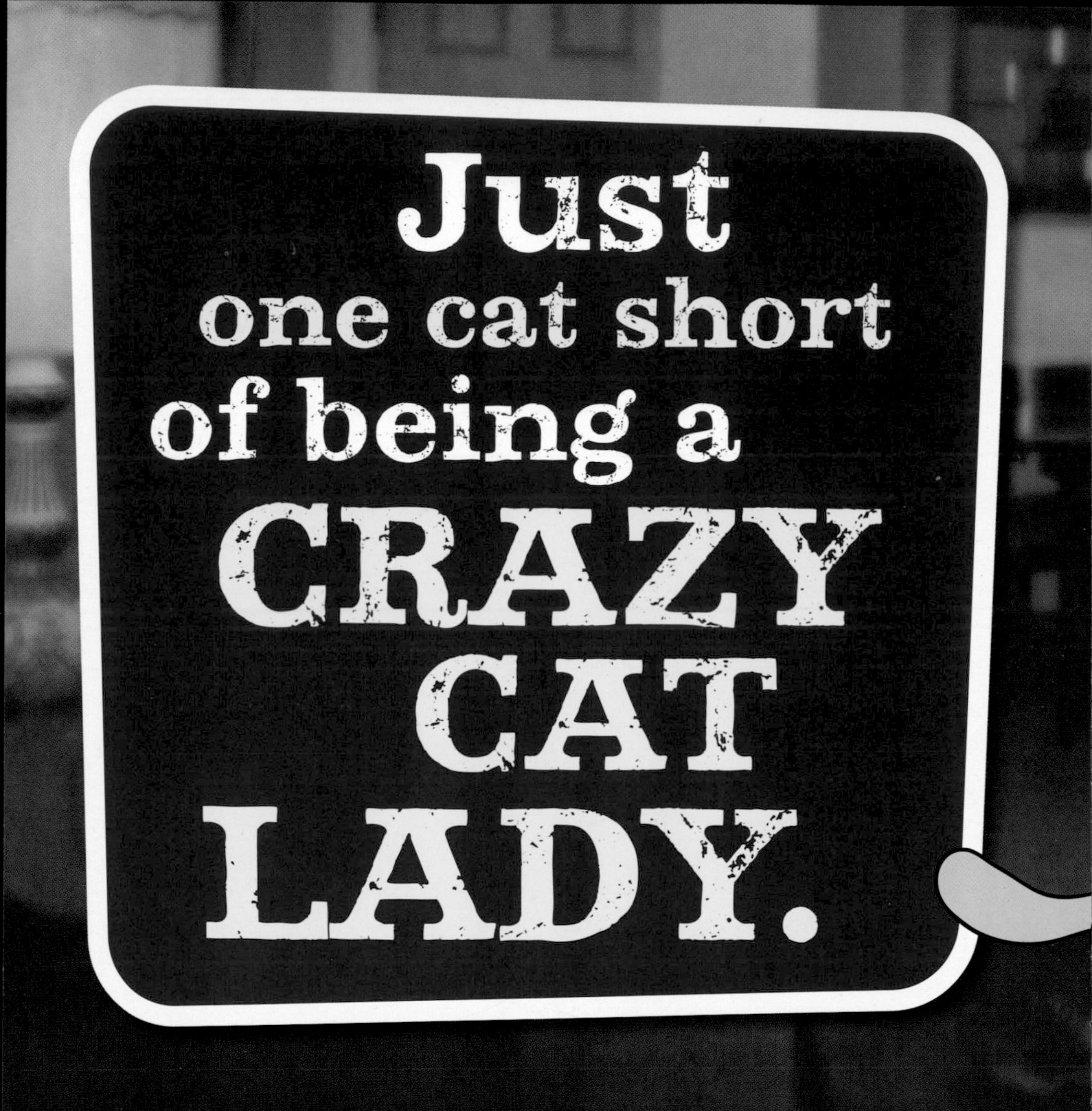
Just
one cat short
of being a
CRAZY
CAT
LADY.

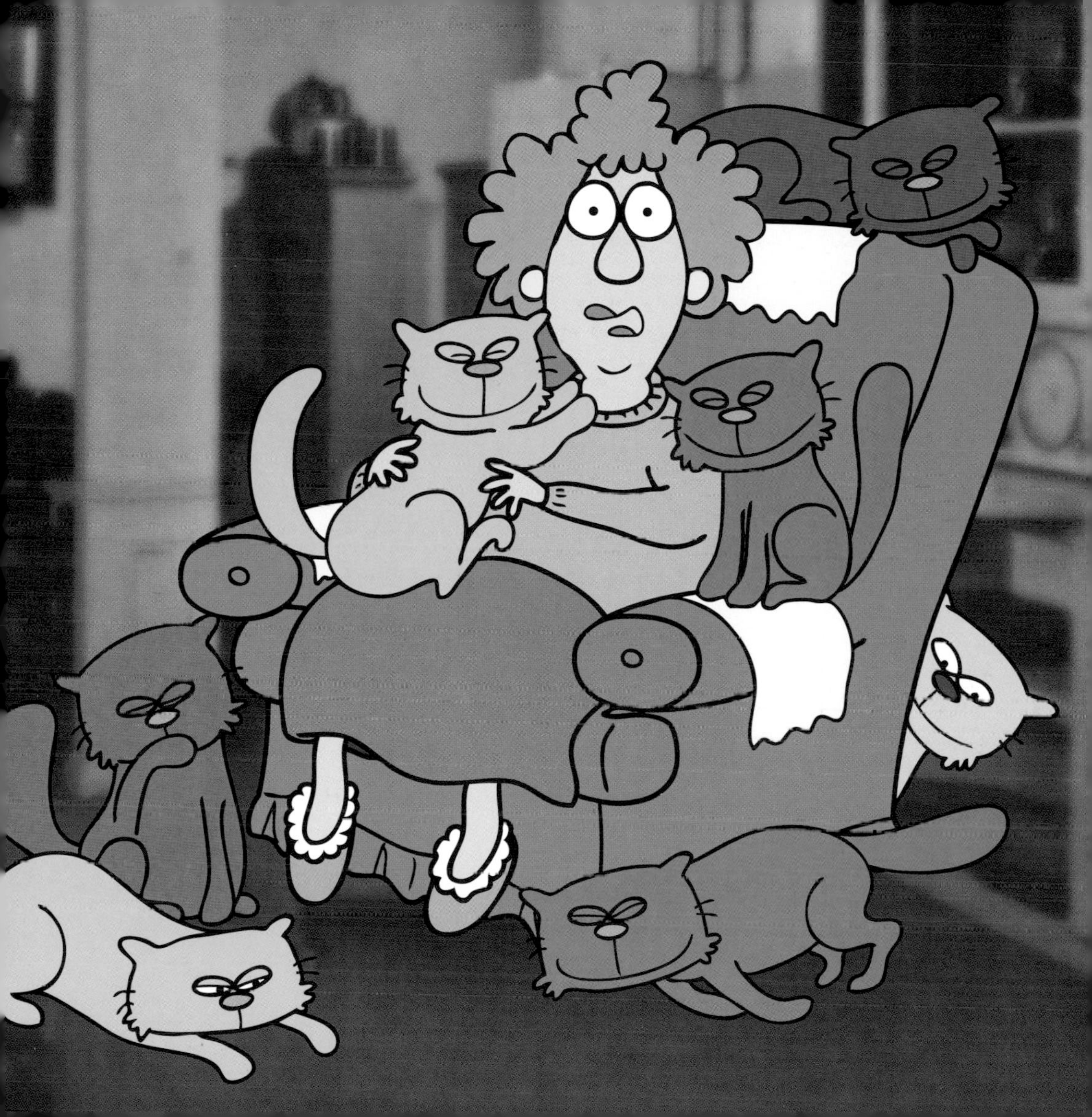

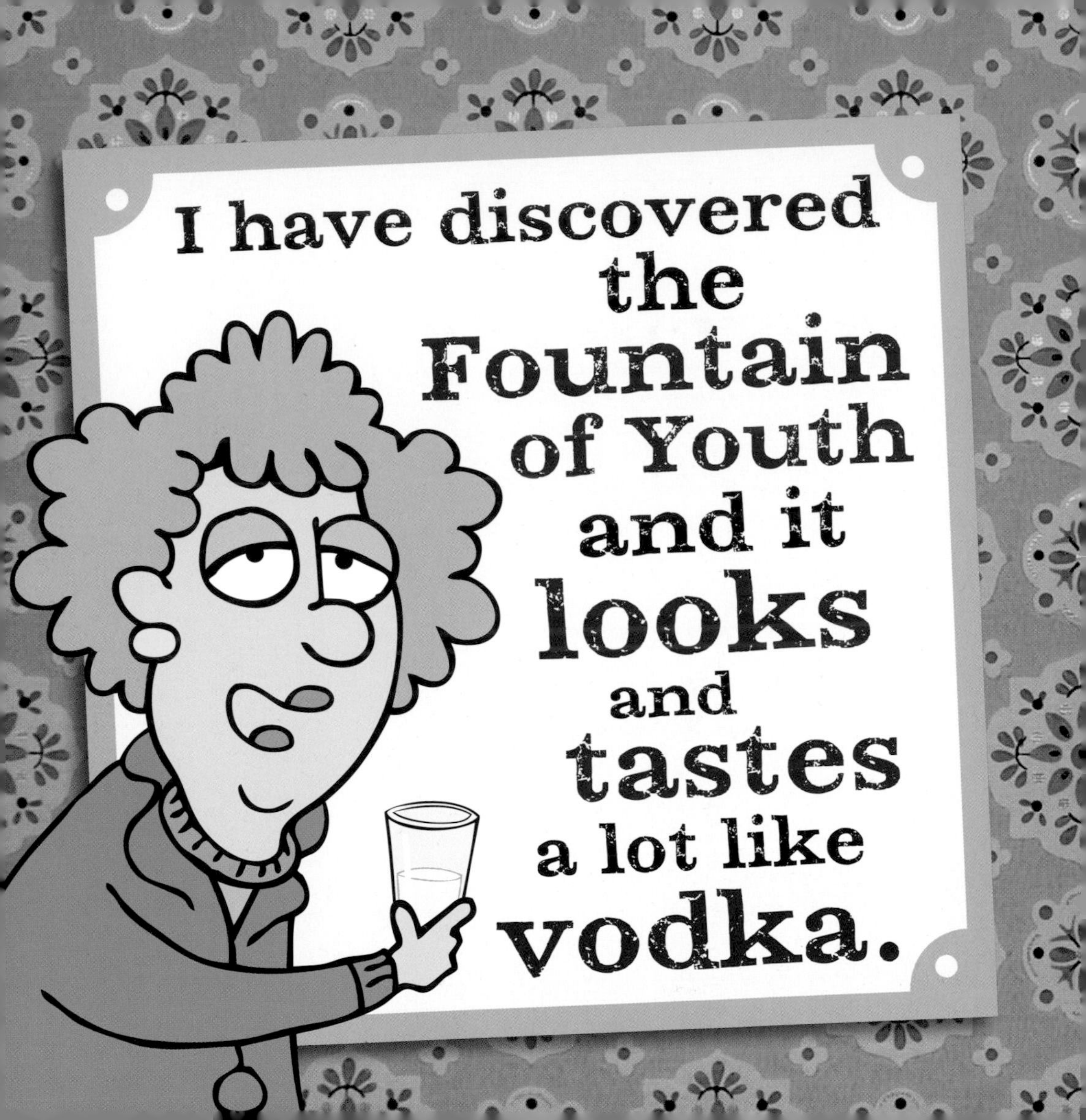
I have discovered the Fountain of Youth and it looks and tastes a lot like vodka.

I'm going to be very busy in the AFTERLIFE. The list of people I'm going to HAUNT grows every day.

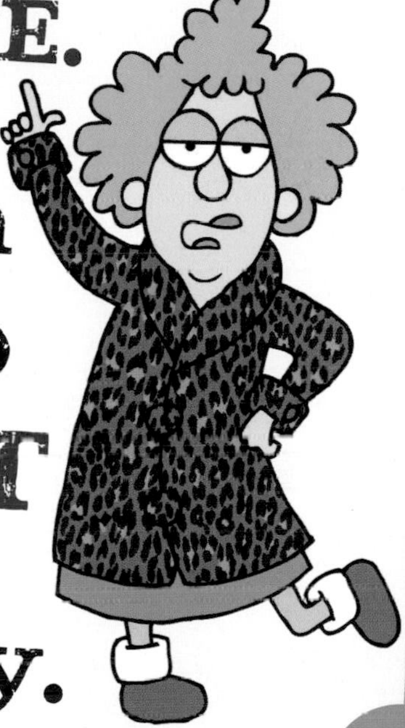

I decided to go for a jog today...

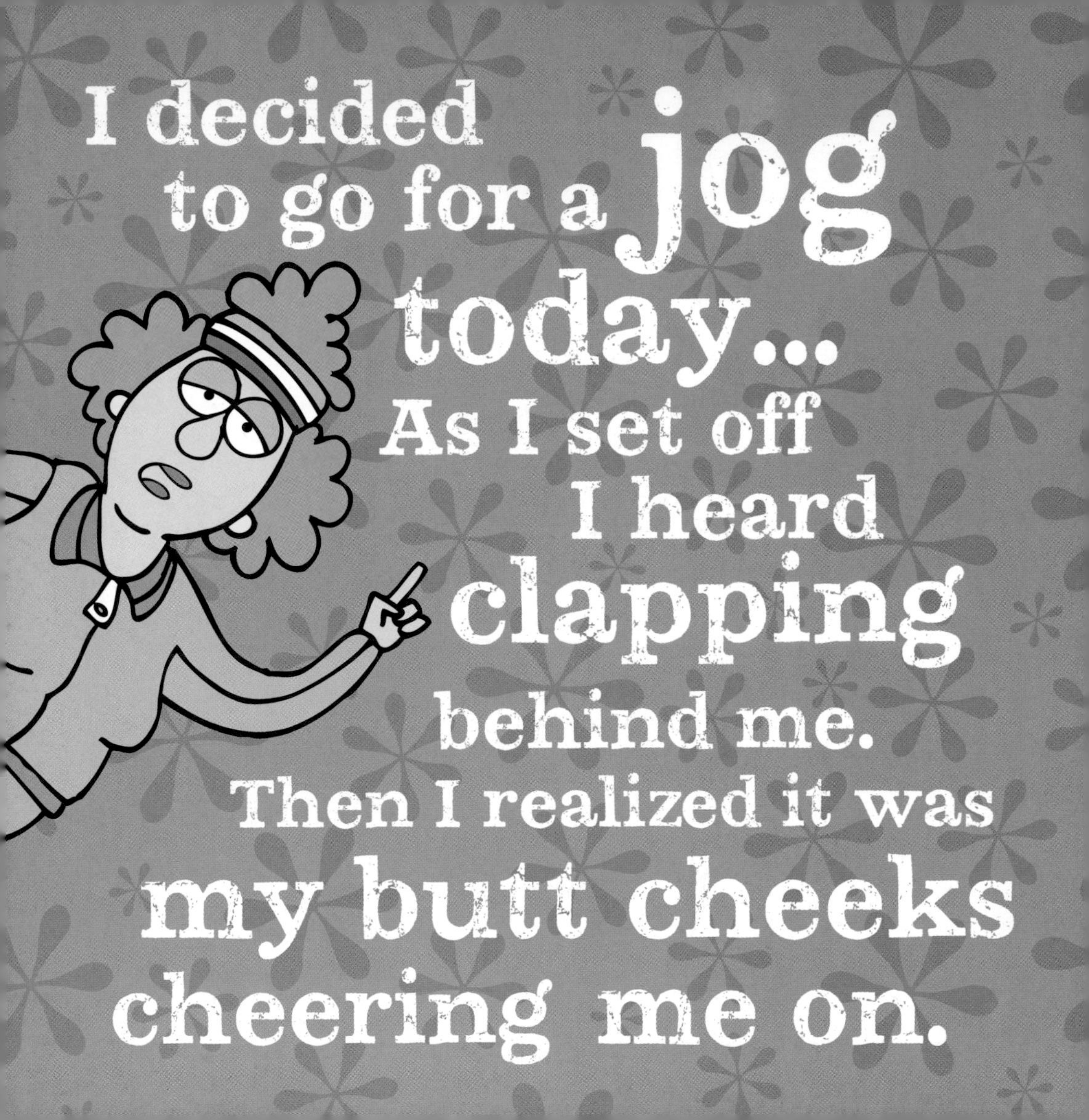

As I set off I heard clapping behind me.

Then I realized it was my butt cheeks cheering me on.

Don't take life too seriously. It's not like you're going to get out alive.

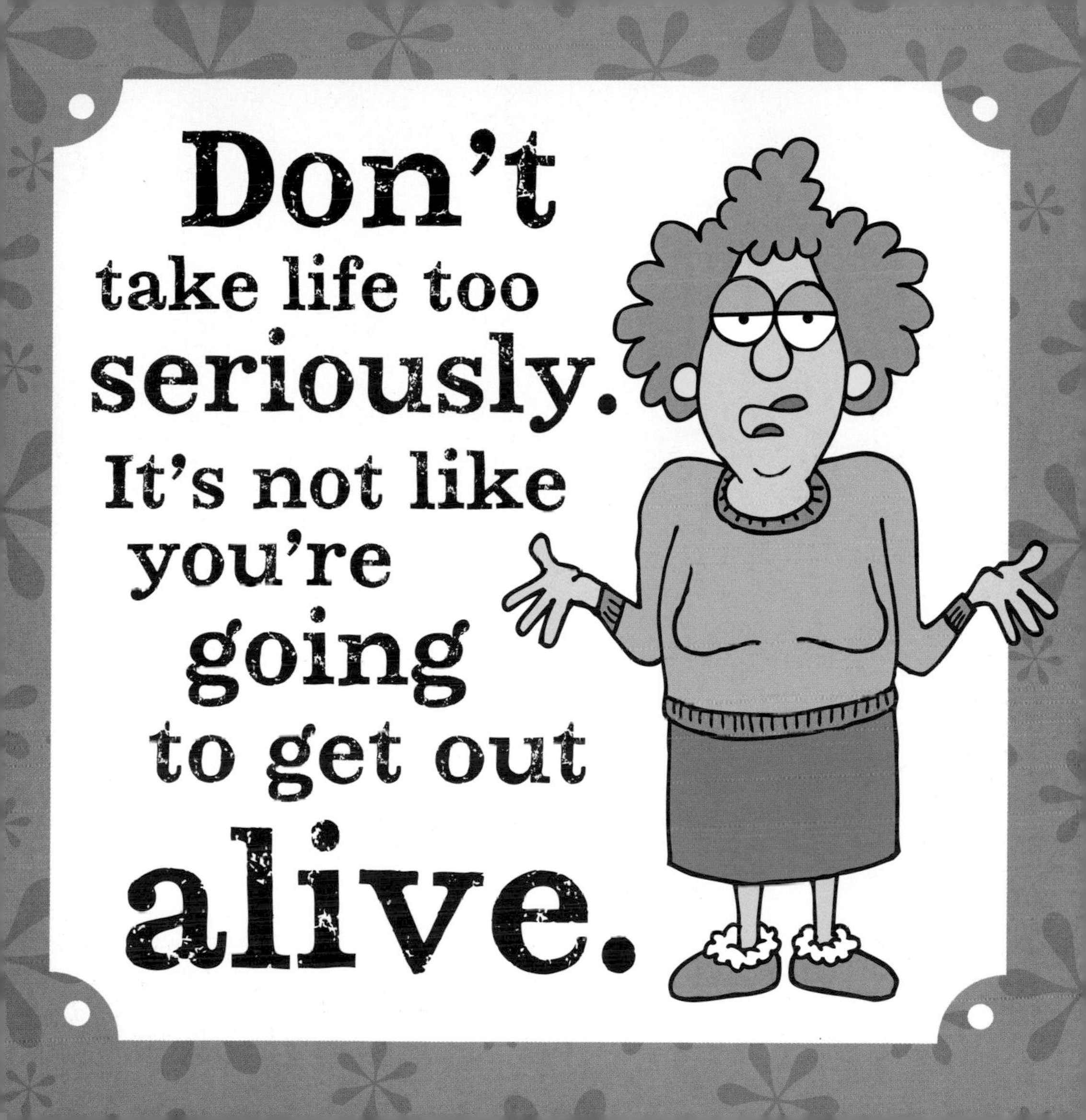

It's bad news

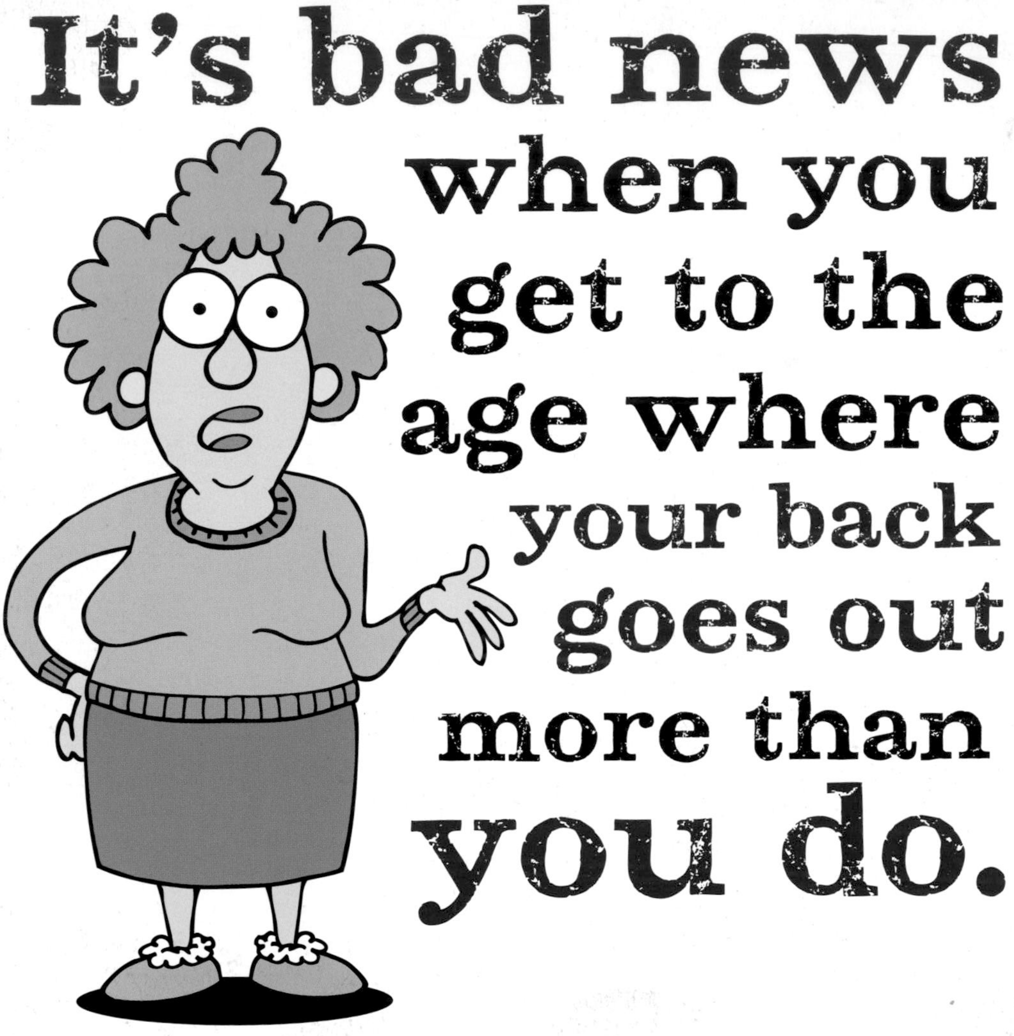

when you get to the age where your back goes out more than you do.

You know you're

getting old

when you get "butt jiggle," "bingo wing flap" and "boob wobble" when you brush your teeth.

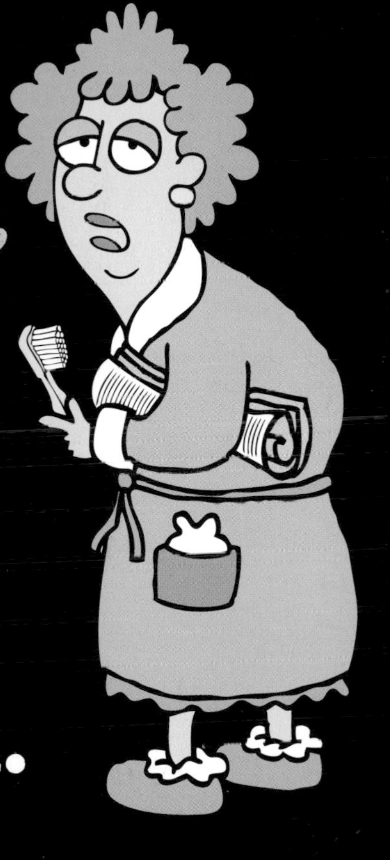

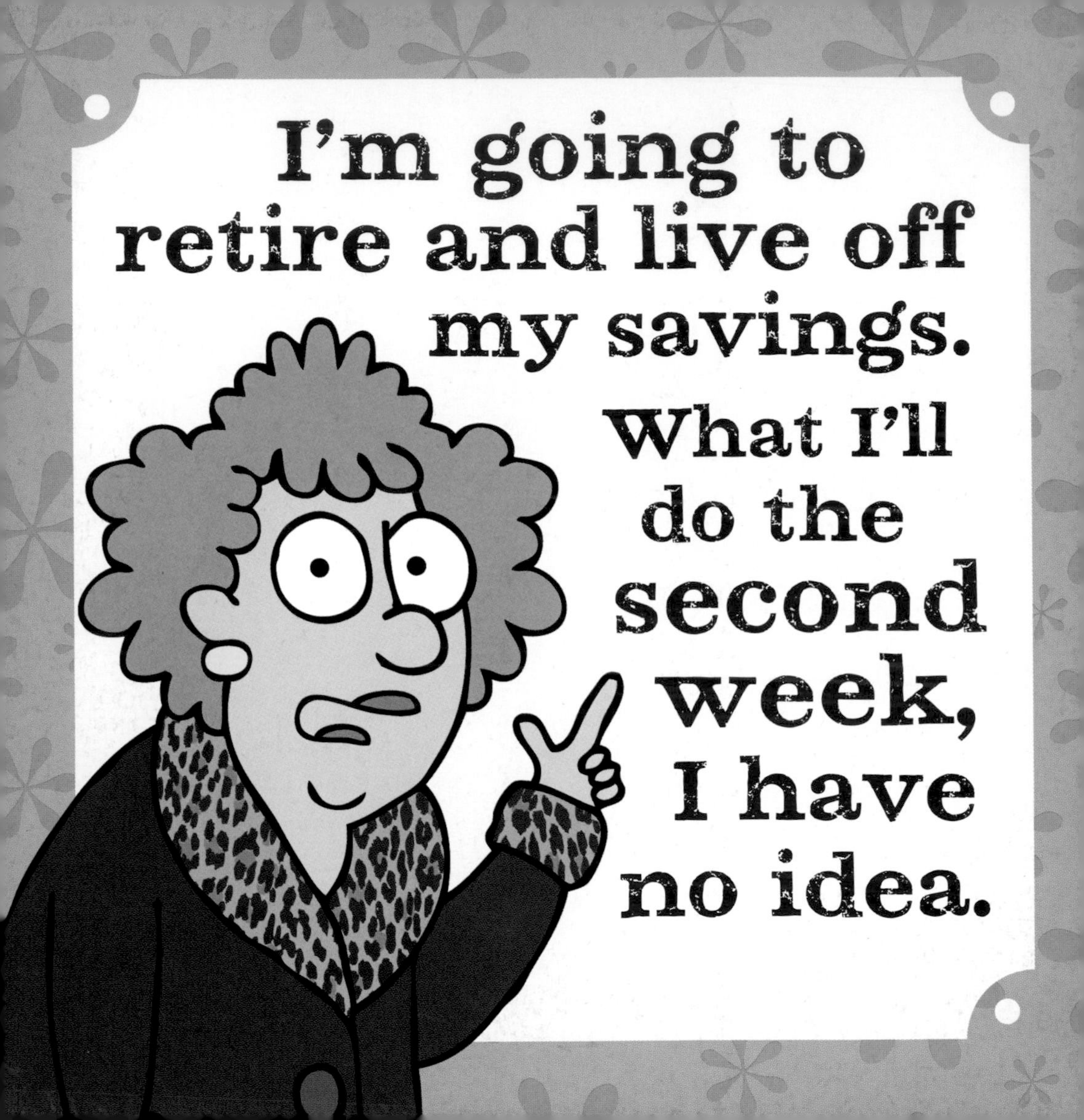
I'm going to retire and live off my savings.
What I'll do the second week, I have no idea.

I don't feel

old.

I don't feel anything until noon. Then it's time for my nap.

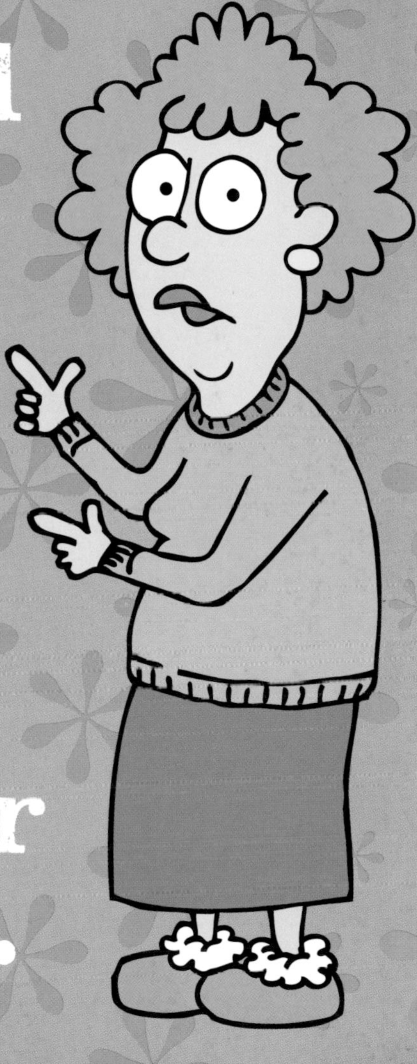

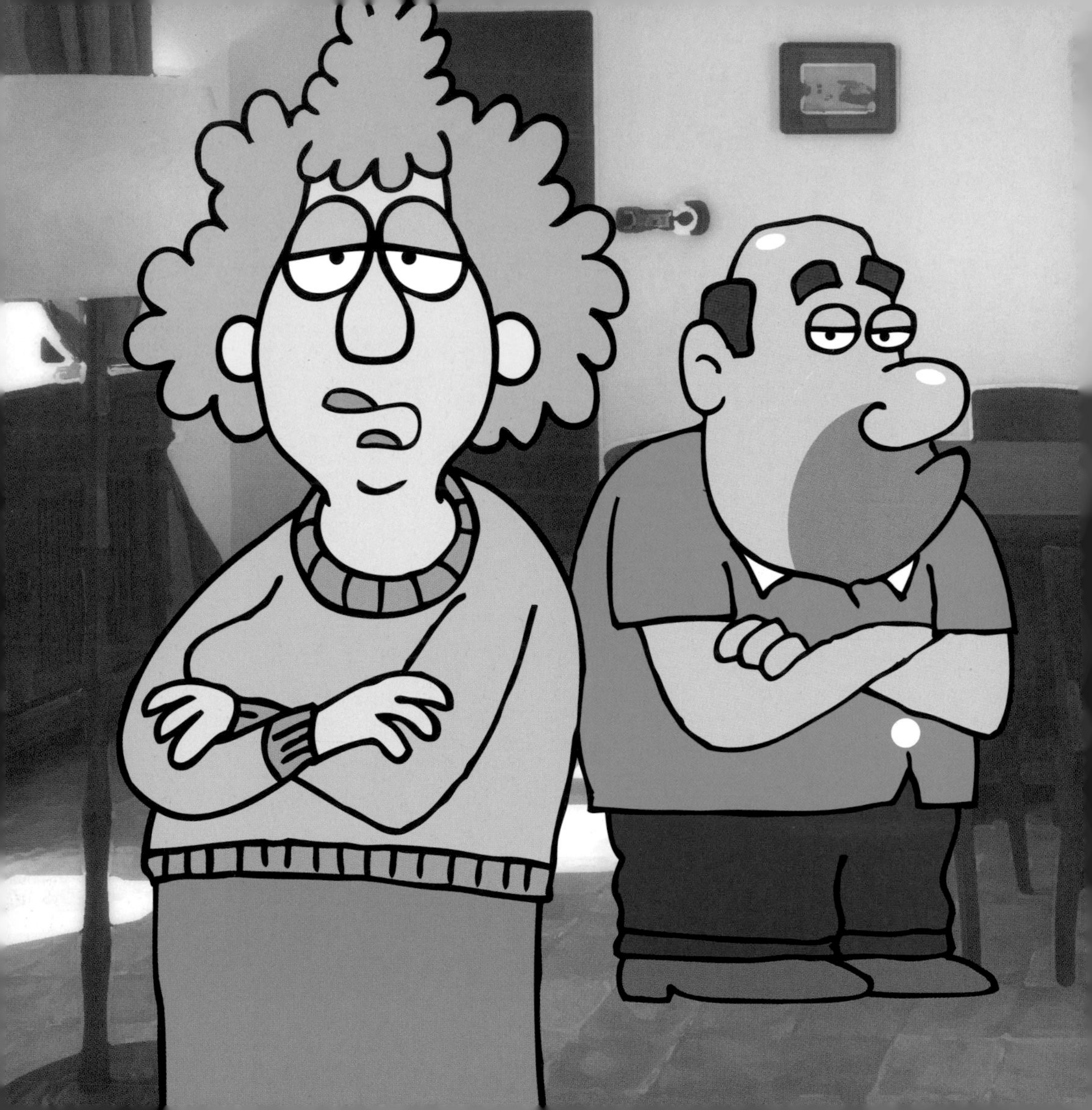

People think it's **romantic** when me and my husband call each other, "Sweety" and "Honey." **Truth is,** we've just forgotten **each other's names.**

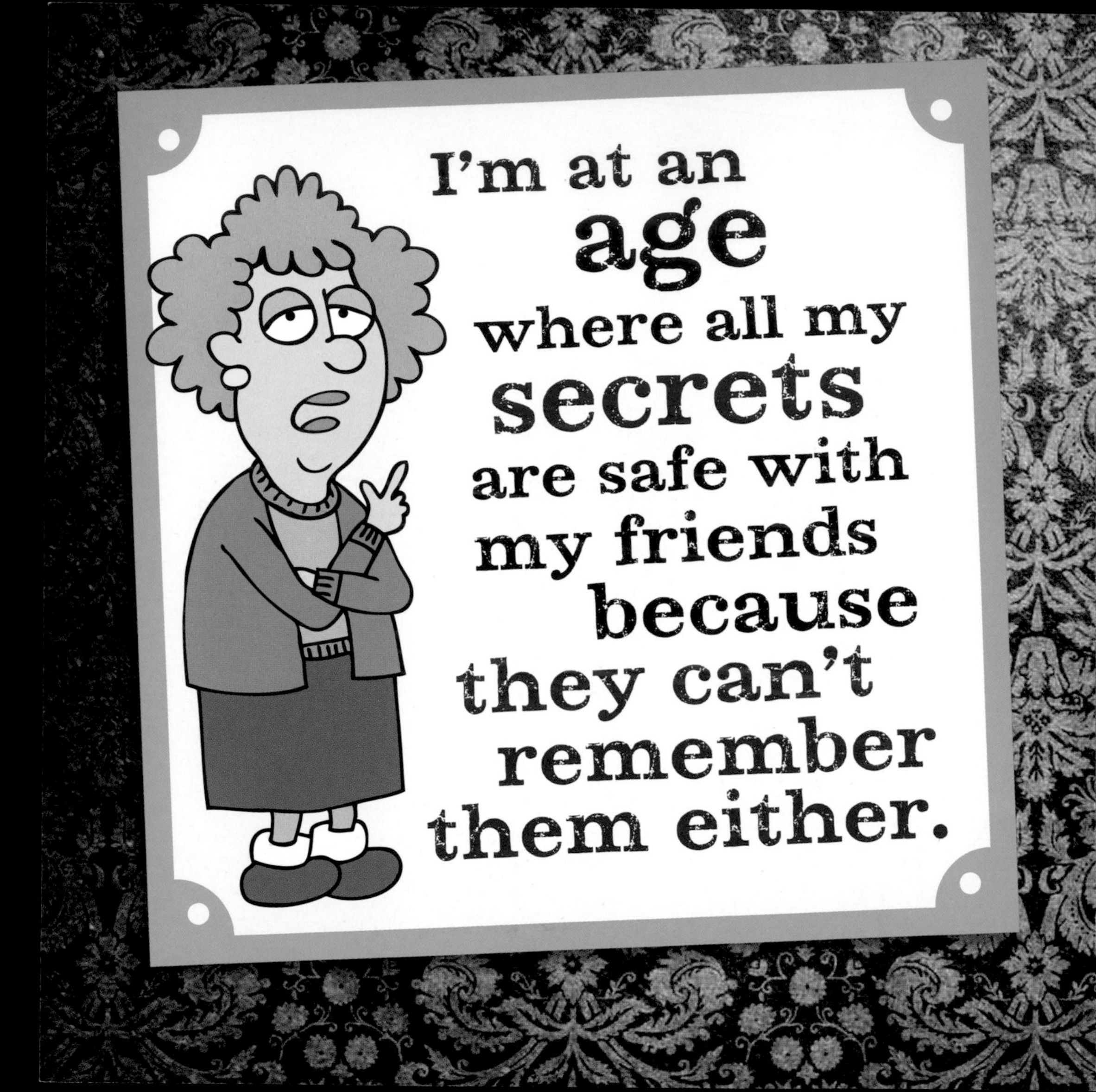

I'm at an
age
where all my
secrets
are safe with
my friends
because
they can't
remember
them either.

Wouldn't
it be
great
if we could
put ourselves
in the dryer
for 10 minutes
and come out
wrinkle
free?

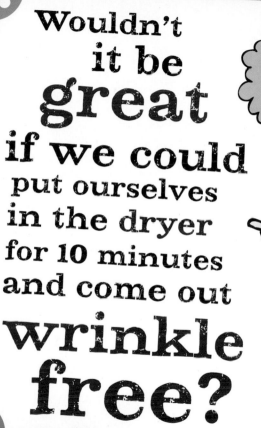

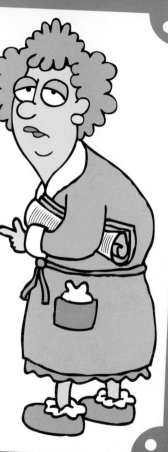

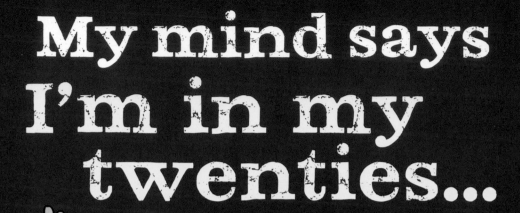

My mind says I'm in my twenties... My body says, "Yeah, you wish!"

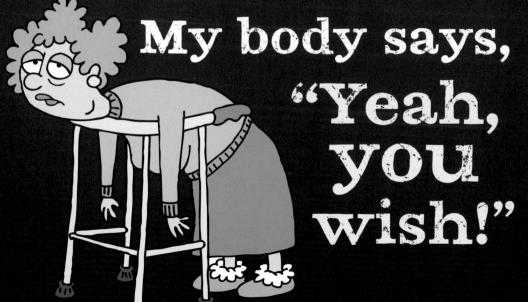

When I was young

I was afraid of
the dark.
Now, when I get
my energy bill,
I'm afraid
of the
freakin'
light.

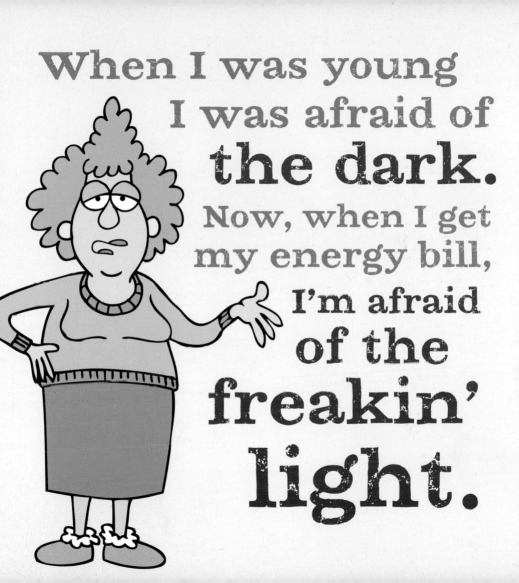

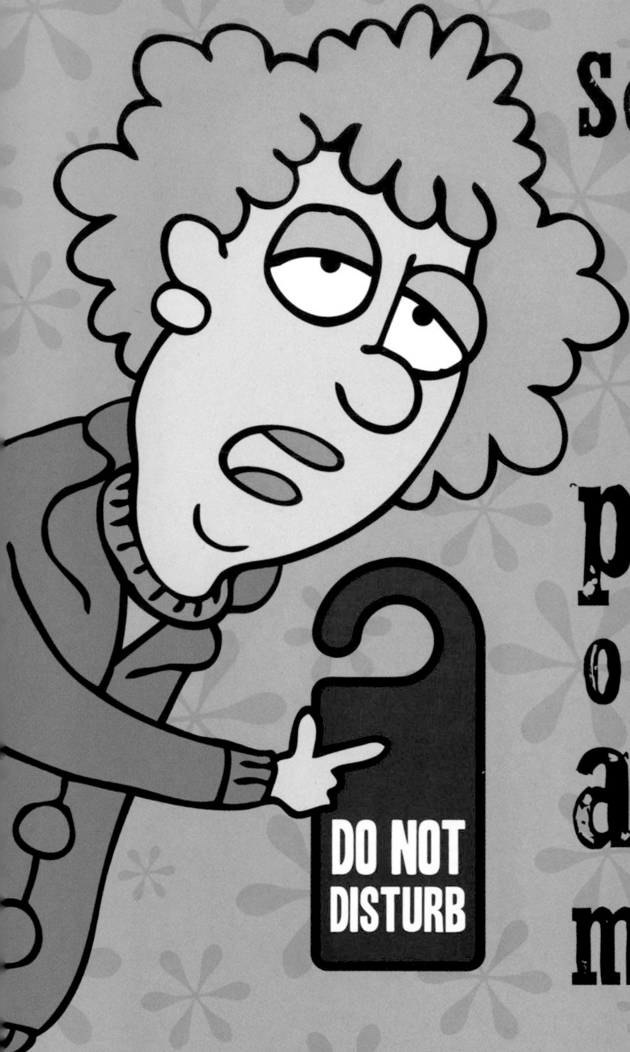
DO NOT
DISTURB

Some days I wish I could put one of these around my neck.

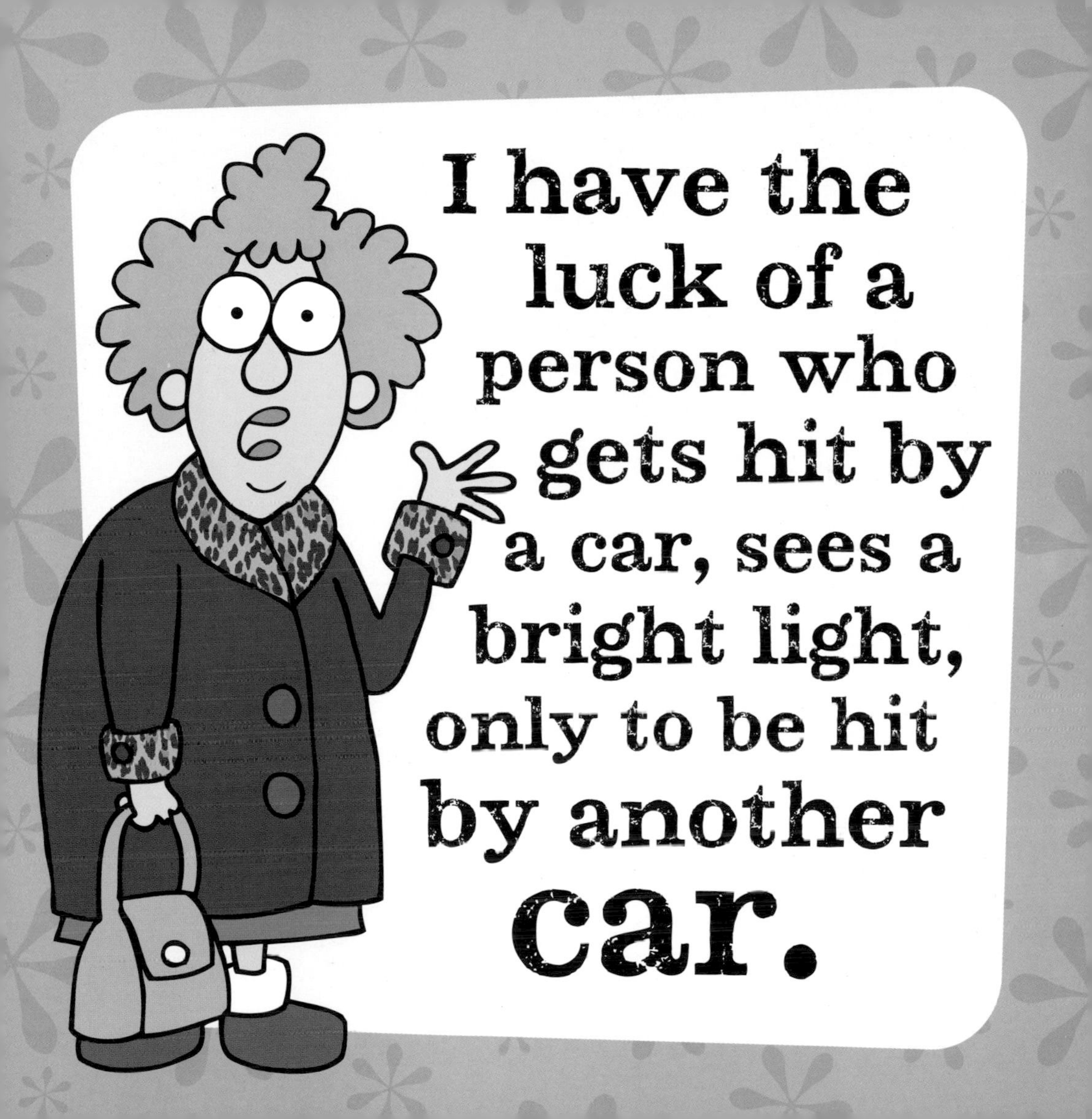

I have the luck of a person who gets hit by a car, sees a bright light, only to be hit by another car.

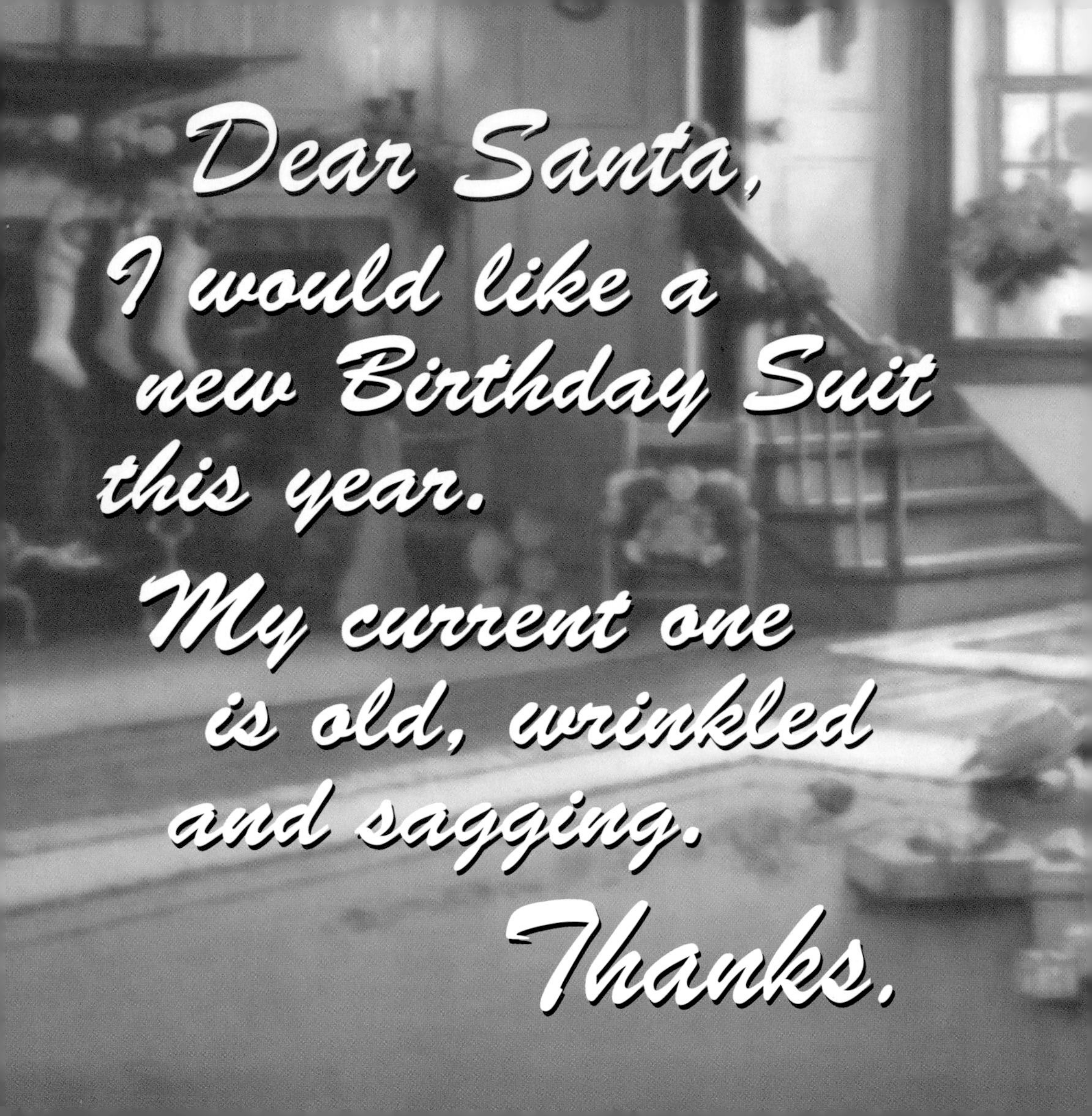
Dear Santa,
I would like a
new Birthday Suit
this year.
My current one
is old, wrinkled
and sagging.
Thanks.

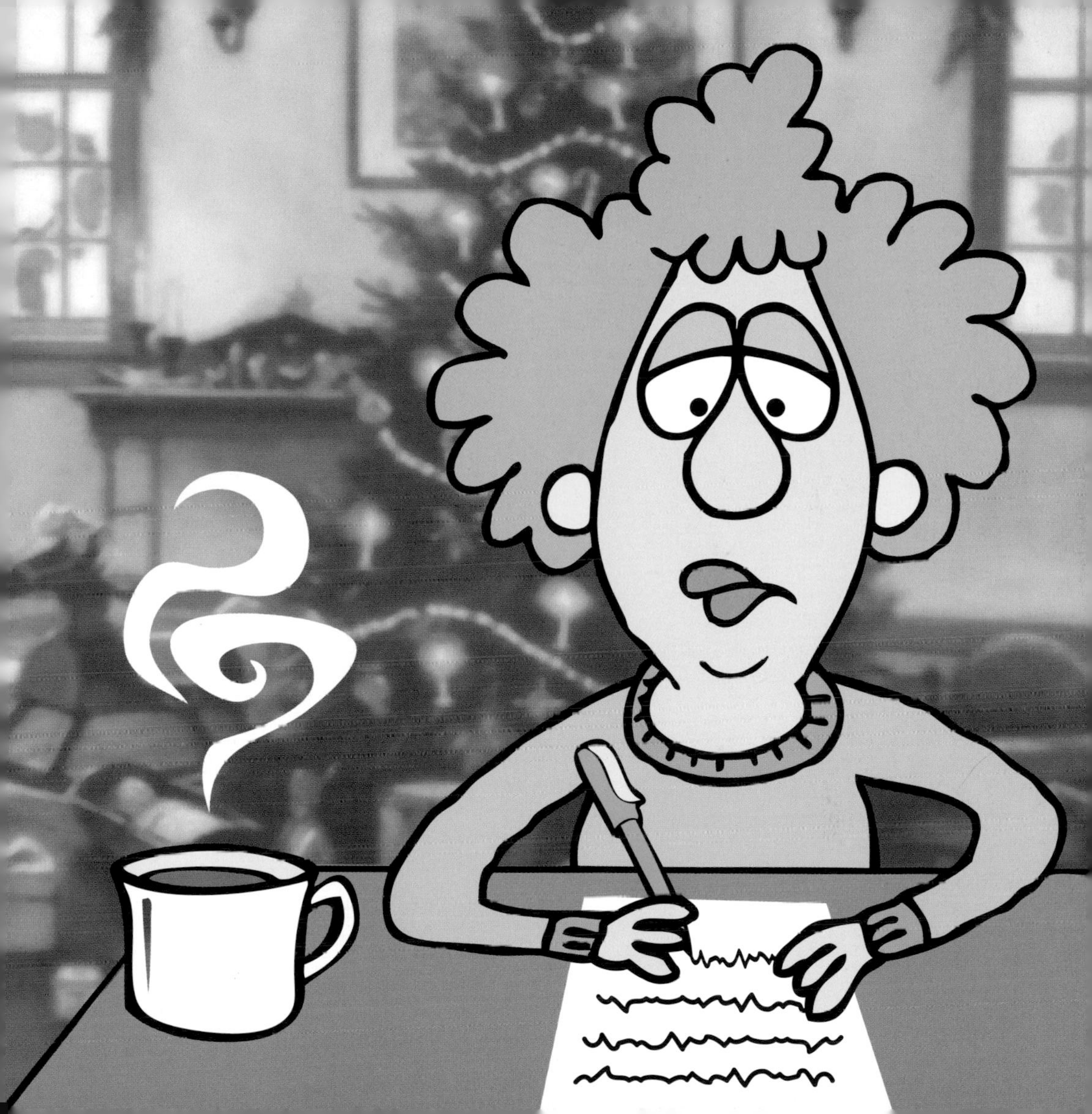

I have a perfect body. It's your vision that's defective.

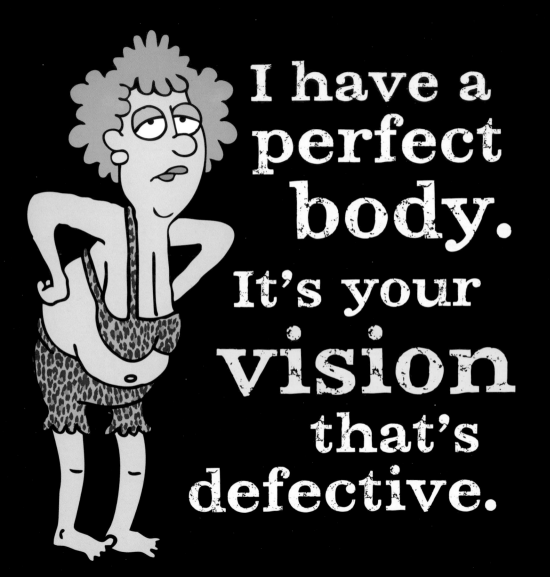

We had "Social Networking" back in the day.

It was called, "Go outside and play."

At my age, rolling out of bed in the morning is easy... Getting up off the floor is another story.

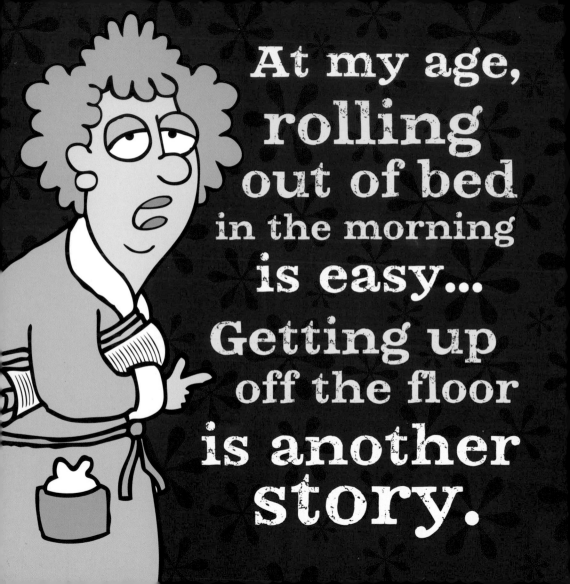

I can't be
over the hill,
I'm too tired
to climb
the
freakin'
stairs.

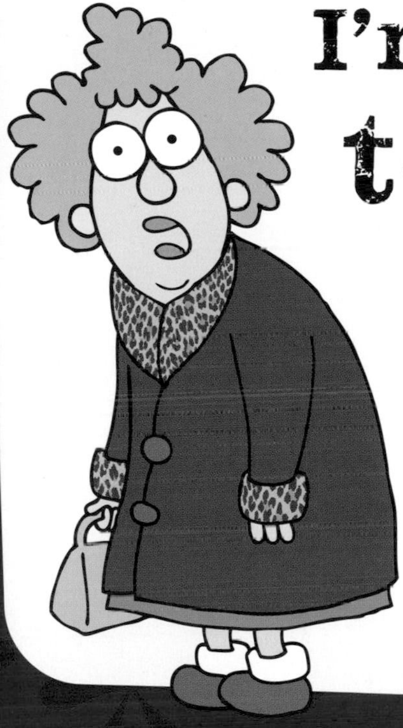

You never realize what you've **GOT** 'til it's **GONE...** Toilet paper is a good example.

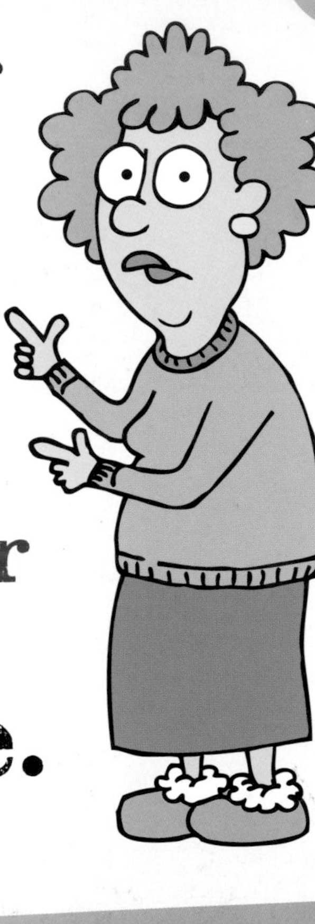

MIRROR MIRROR ON THE WALL... WHAT THE FREAKIN' HELL HAPPENED?

Sure getting older has its perks... I just wish someone would tell that to my boobs and butt! No seriously, I'm so old I can laugh, cough, sneeze and pee all at once. It saves me a lot of freakin' time!

Hey, sometimes I worry that I haven't done enough with my life... Then something good comes on the TV and I'm okay again.

Read on for my witty wisdom on staying wrinkle free, crazy cat ladies and naughty numbers!

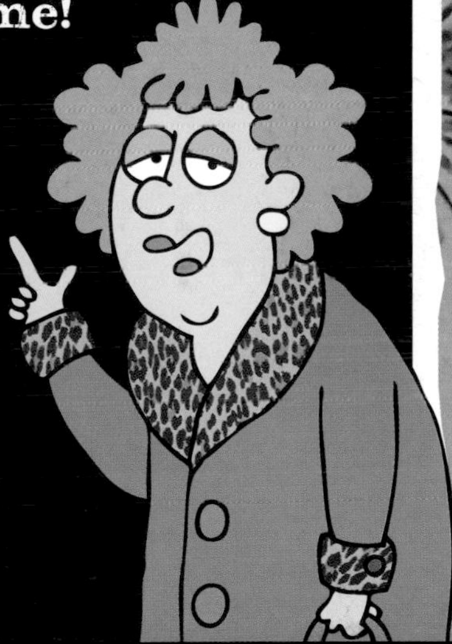

AUNTY ACID'S LIFE TIPS FOR SENIORS No.18

Never,
under any
circumstances,
take a
sleeping pill
and a
laxative
on the
same night.

Whenever I start feeling spontaneous, my bank account quietly reminds me to calm the hell down.

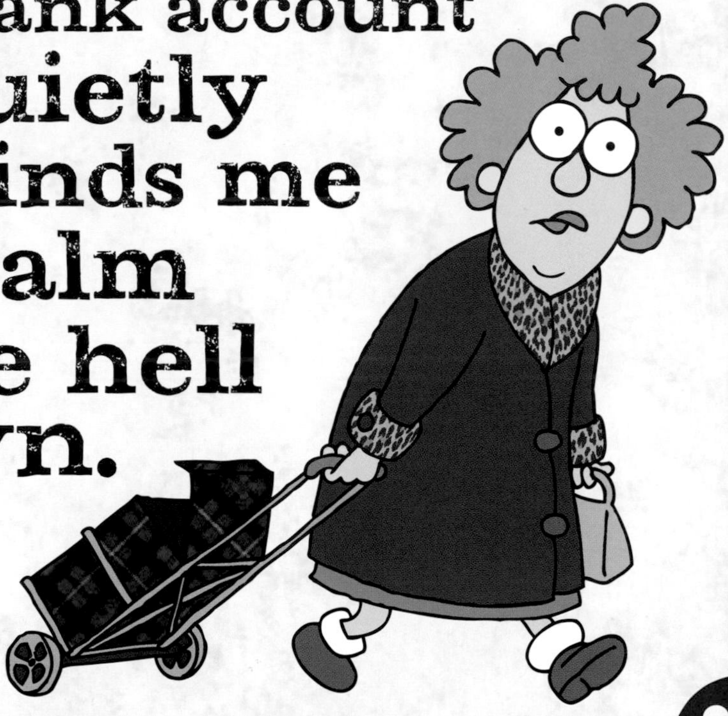

I've forgotten some of the men in my life... but I remember ALL the cats.

Rise?
...if I must.
Shine?
...it ain't freakin' happening.

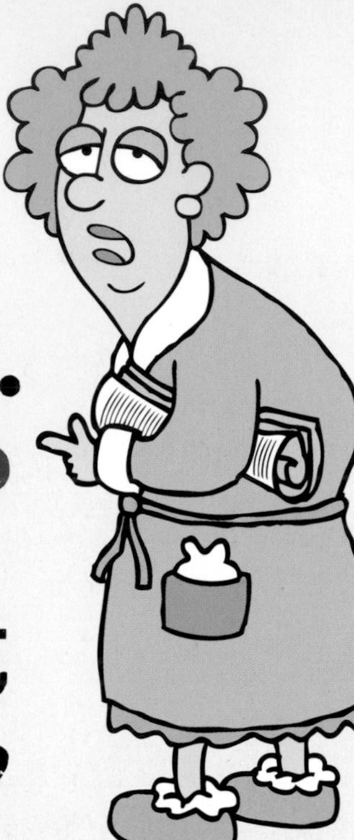

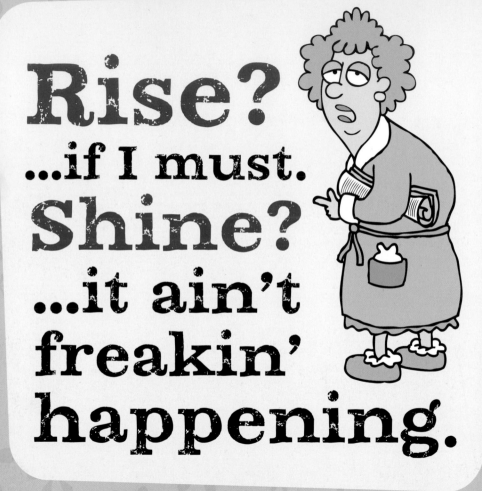

I went to a male strip club last night and this hunk sat on my knee and offered me "SUPER SEX."

I said, "At my age, dear, I'd better stick with the soup."

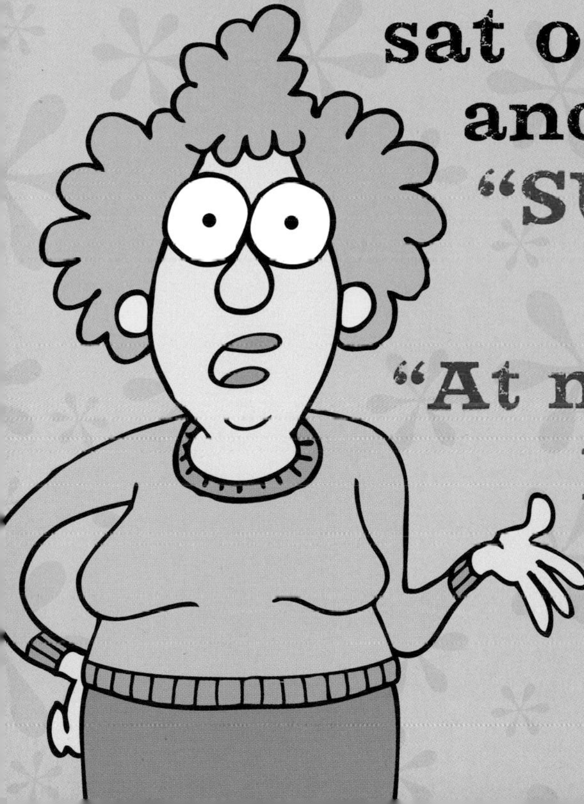

AUNTY ACID'S TE[redacted]T CODE FOR SENIORS

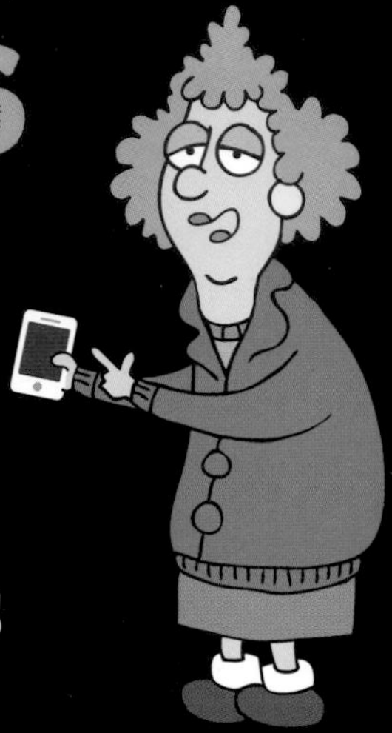

ATD - At The Doctor's
BFF - Best Friend Fell
BTW - Bring The Wheelchair
BYOT - Bring Your Own Teeth
FWI[redacted] - Forgot Where I Was
GHA [redacted] Got Heartburn Again
IMHO - Is My Hearing Aid On
TTYL - Talk To You Louder
LMDO - Laughing My Dentures Out

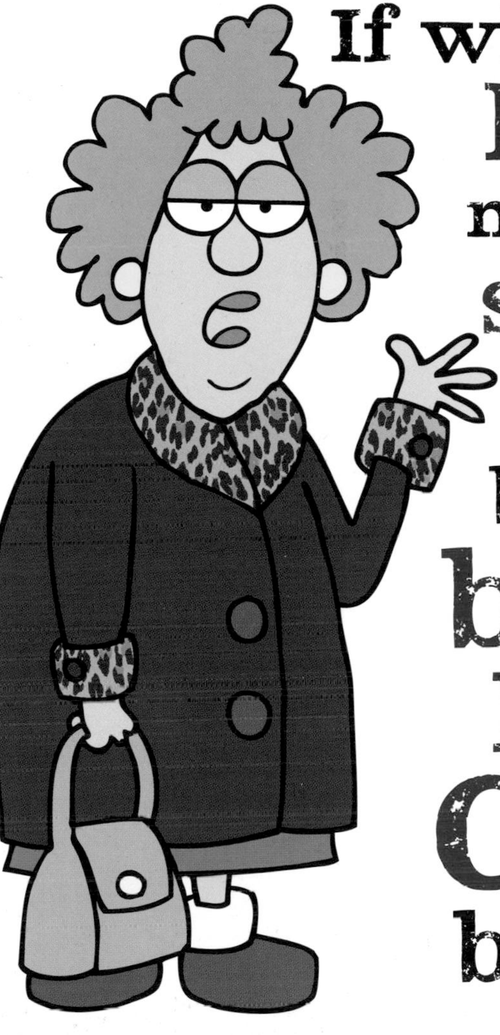

If what doesn't
kill you
makes you
stronger,
I should
be able to
bench
press a
Cadillac
by now.

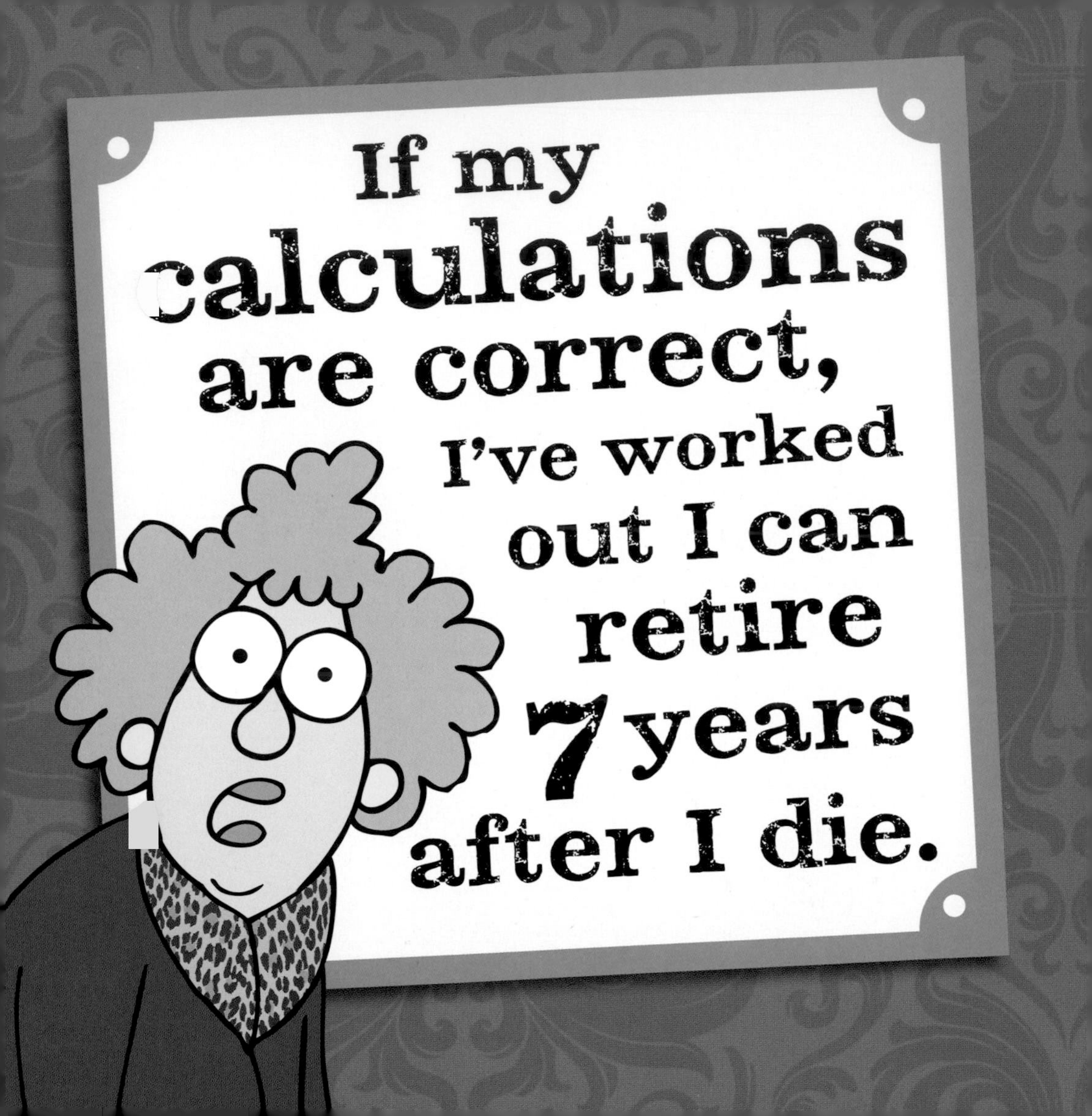
If my calculations are correct, I've worked out I can retire 7 years after I die.

There should be a children's song:

"If you're happy and you know it... keep it to yourself and let Grandma sleep."

Beautiful people and ugly people basically look the same by 80...

So us uglies have just got to hang on in there.

When I die, I've told Walt I want to be buried face down. So everyone can kiss my sweet lily white ass.

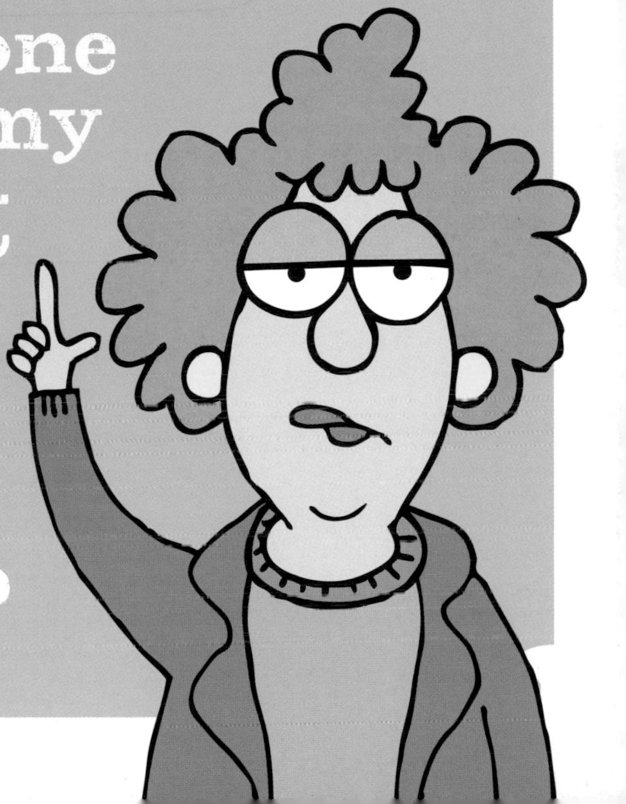

Age

is only a
number.

Weight

is only a
number.

I've decided that numbers are really starting to p*ss me off.

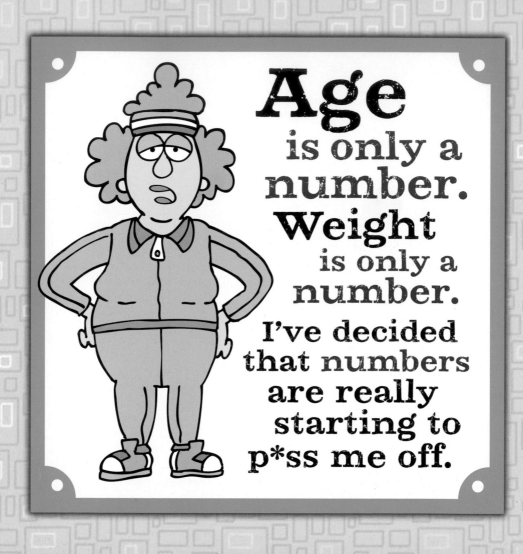

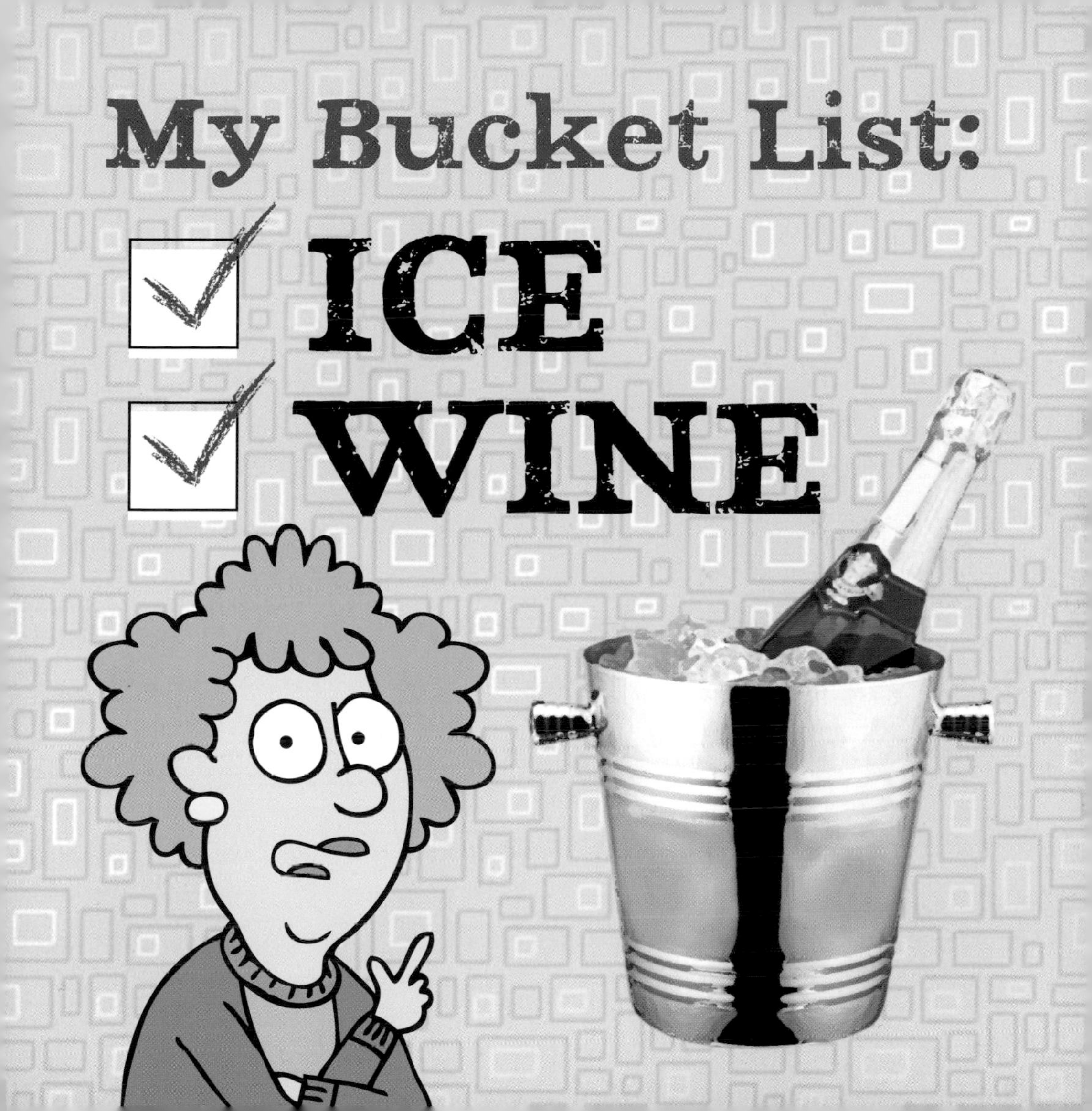
My Bucket List:
ICE
WINE

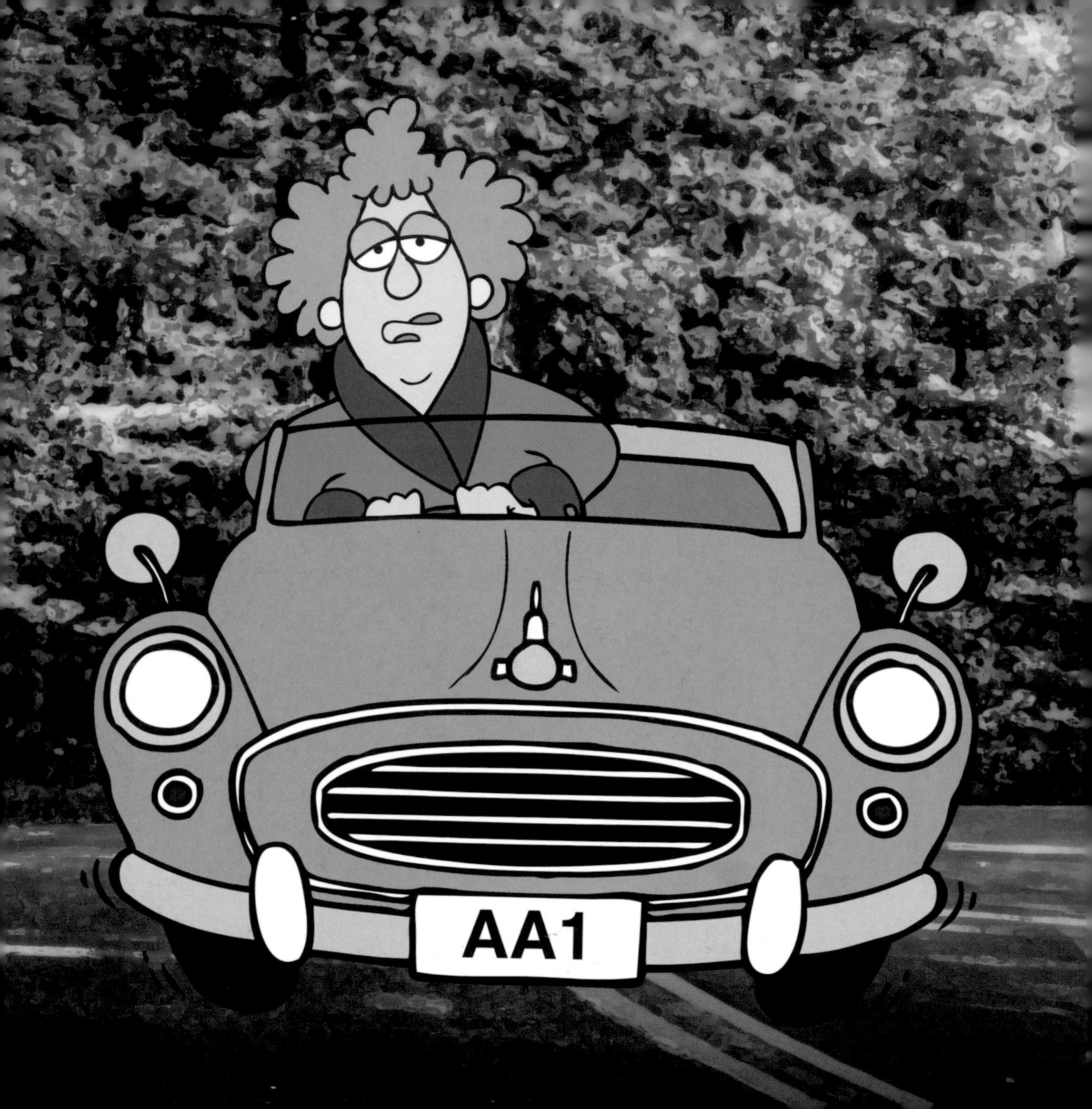
AA1

If my body was a
car,
I'd trade it in for a
newer model.
'Cuz every time
I cough or sneeze,
my radiator leaks
and my **exhaust**
backfires.

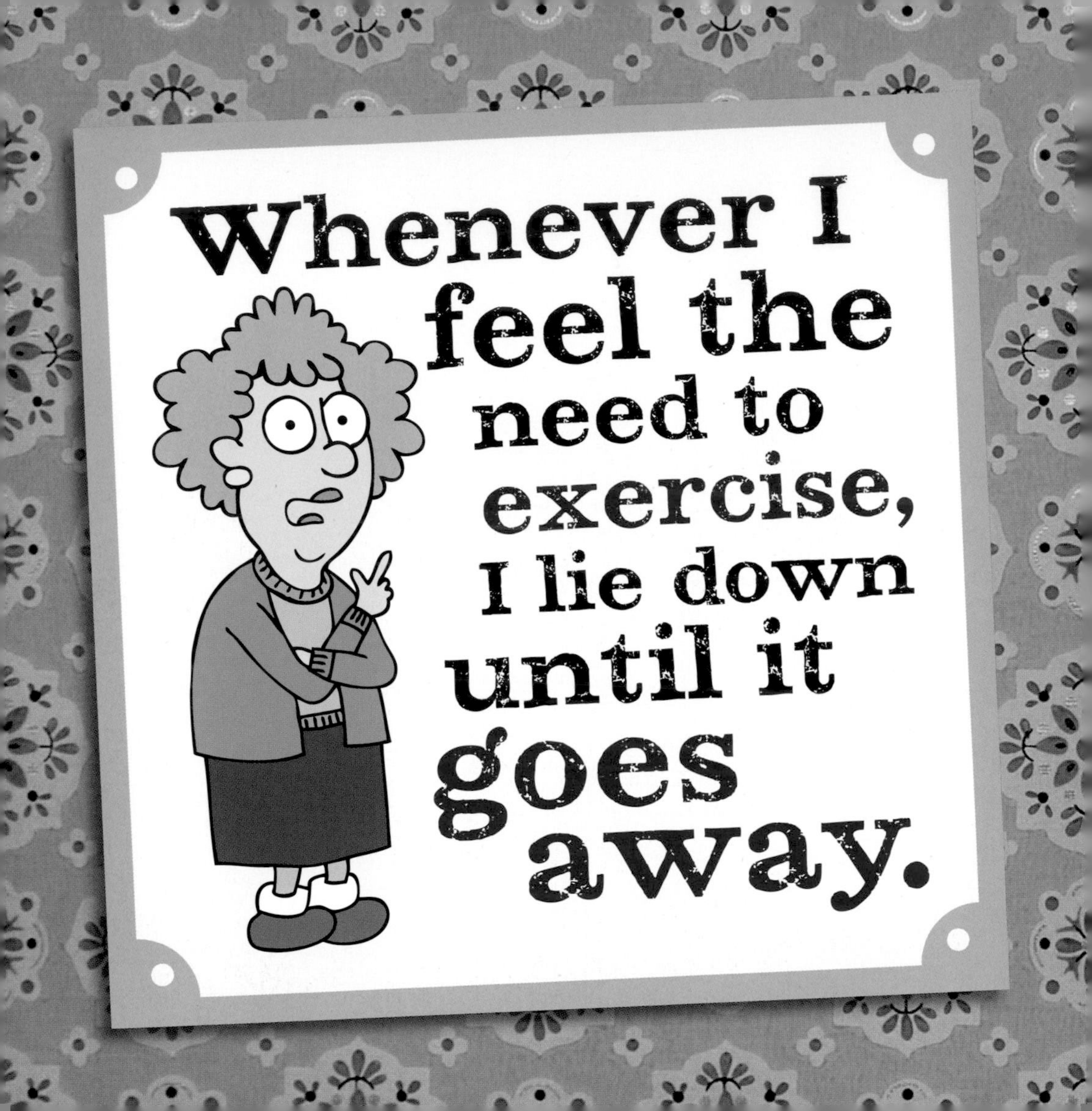
Whenever I feel the need to exercise, I lie down until it goes away.

I'm so tired, the bags under my eyes are bigger than my boobs.

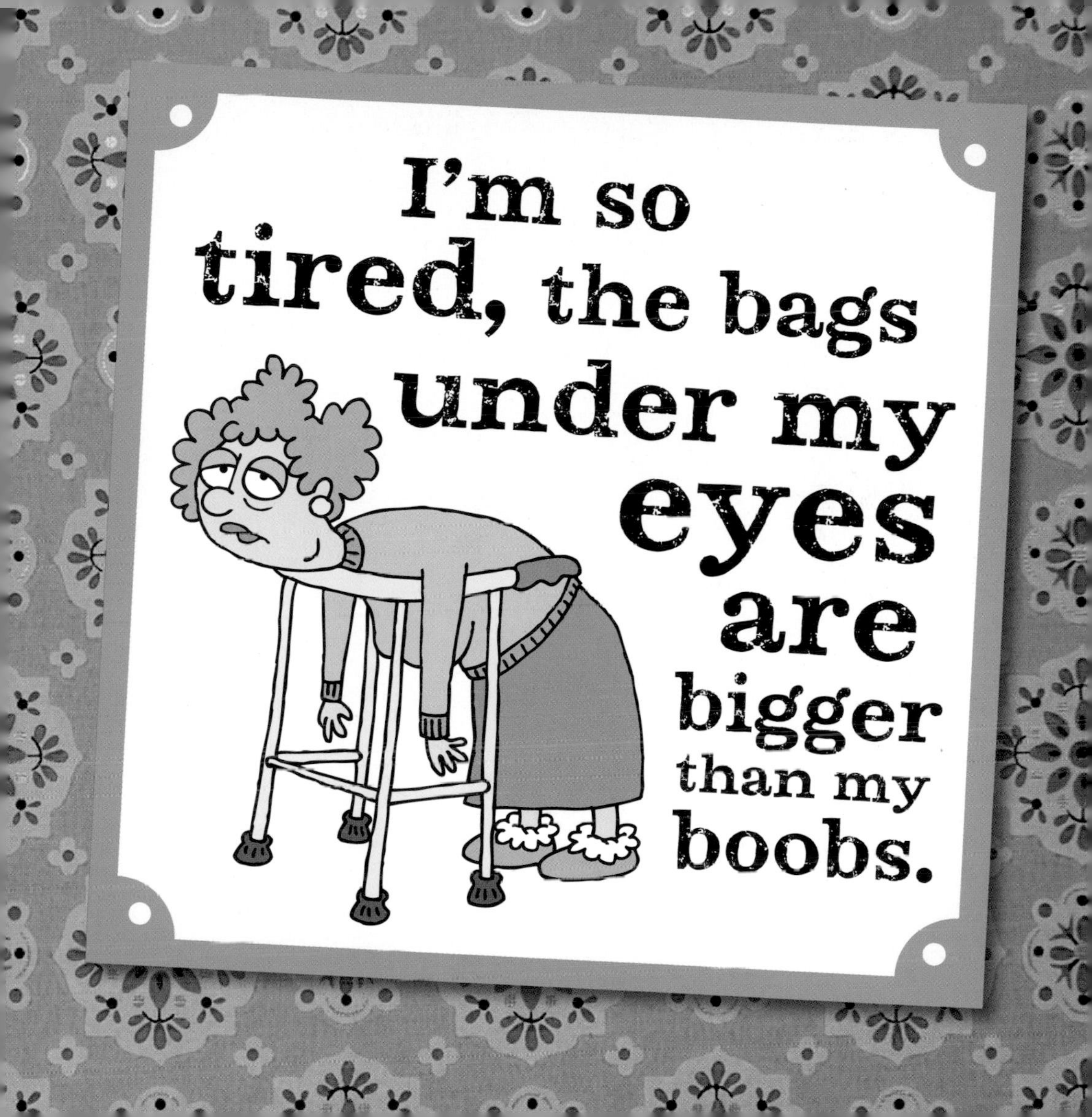

If we learn from our **mistakes...**

I've made so many I should be a **genius** by now.

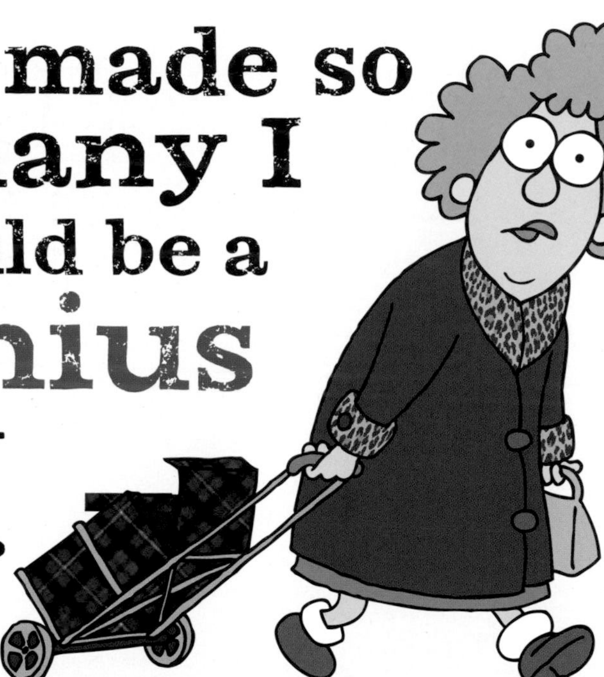

I'm not sure if life is passing me by or trying to run me over.

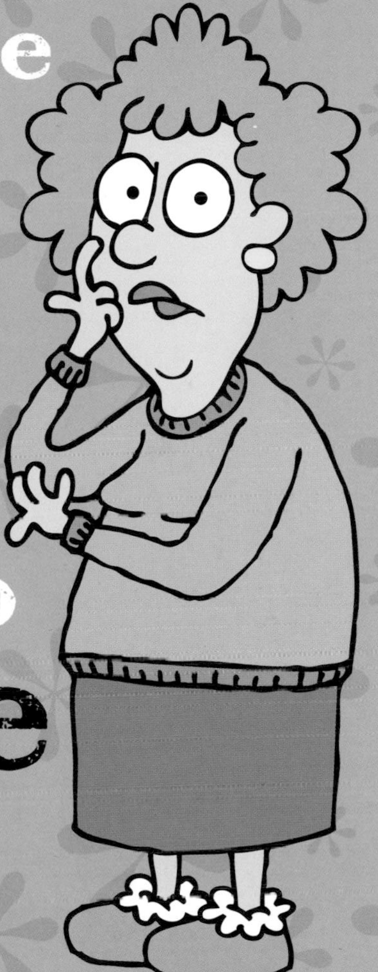

When I pass away,

I'd like them to write the word HUMBLE on my statue.

You know you're gettin' OLD when you can't walk past a bathroom without thinking, "I may as well pee while I'm here."

The 16-minute

WORKOUT

1. Go jog for 1 minute.

2. Lie down in the road for 15 minutes because exercise is freakin' painful.

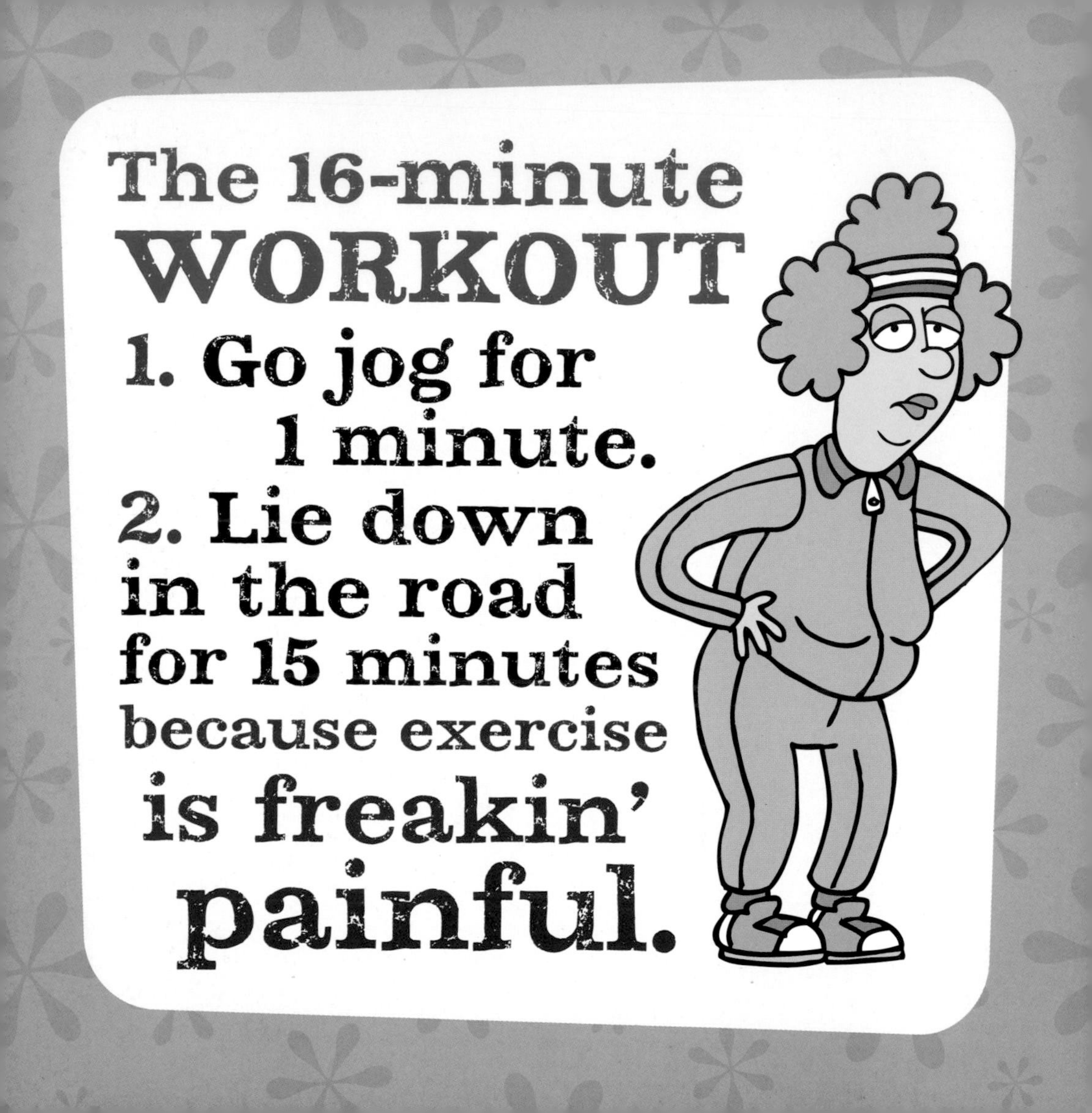

If things get better with age then I must be getting close to freakin' magnificent.

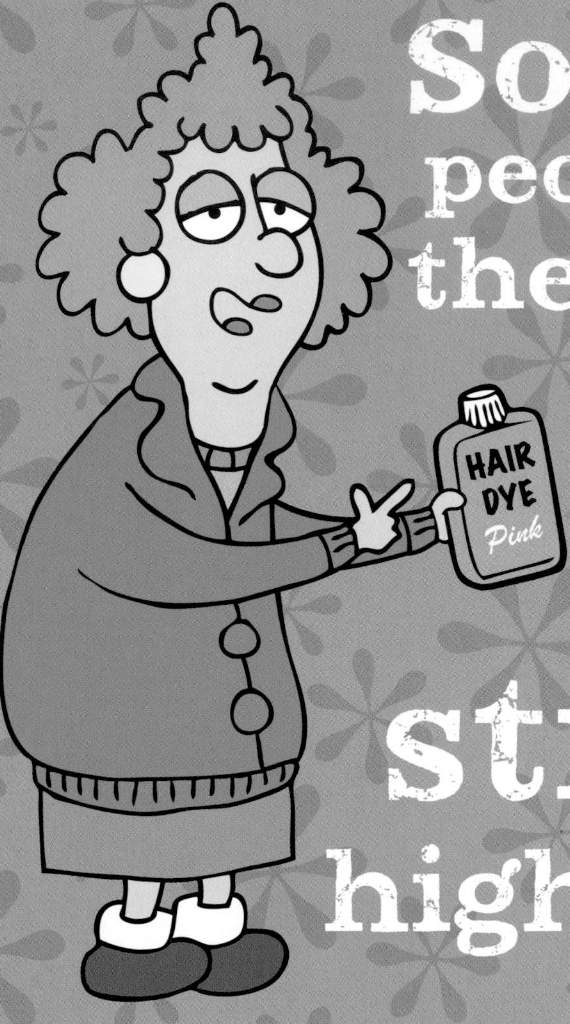
HAIR DYE
Pink

Some people call them gray hairs. I call them stress highlights.

We'll be friends 'til we're old and senile... and then we'll be new friends all over again.

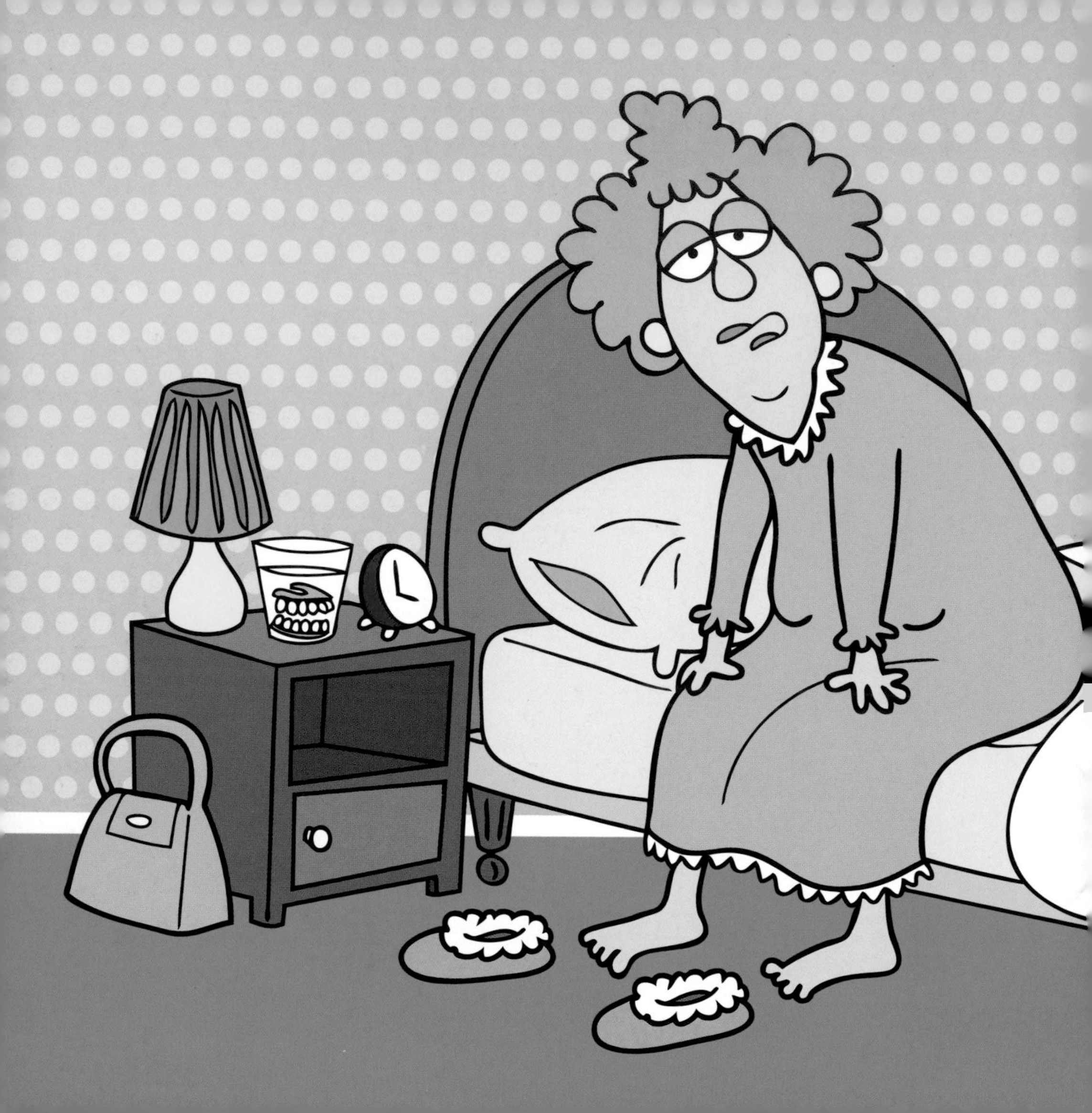

Don't give up on your dreams...
Keep on sleeping.

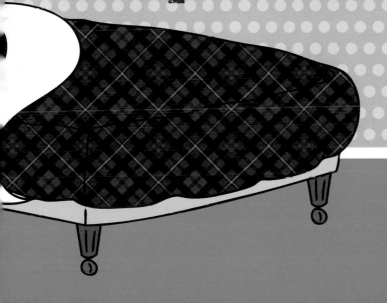

I'm not

FAT.

I'm just so freakin' **SEXY** it overflows.

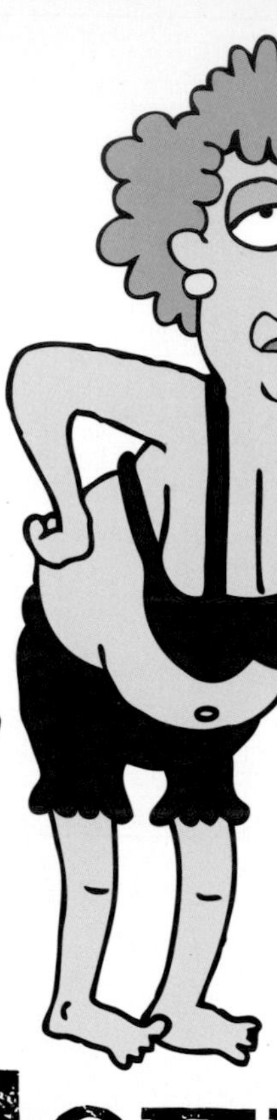

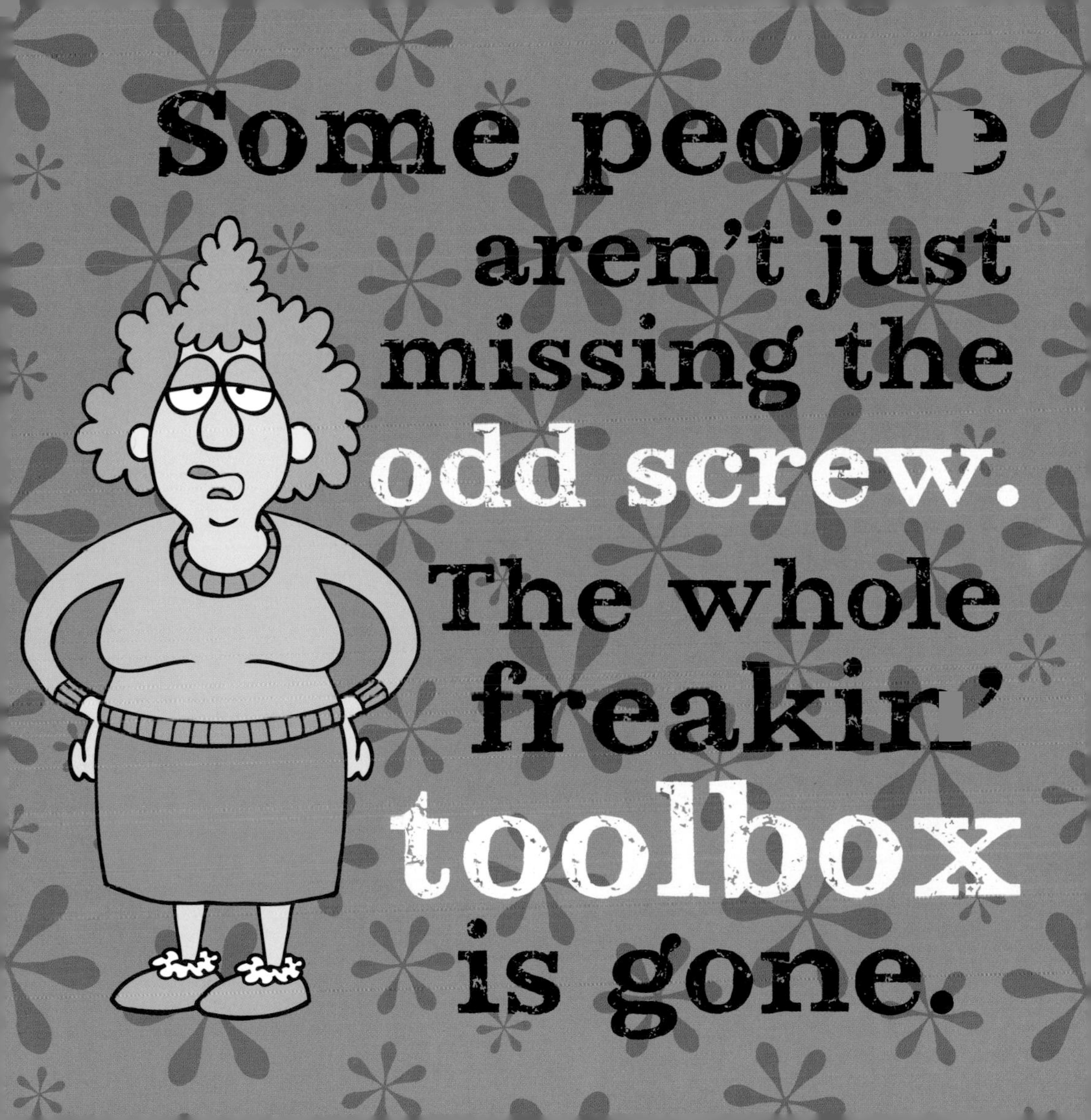

Some people aren't just missing the odd screw. The whole freakin' toolbox is gone.

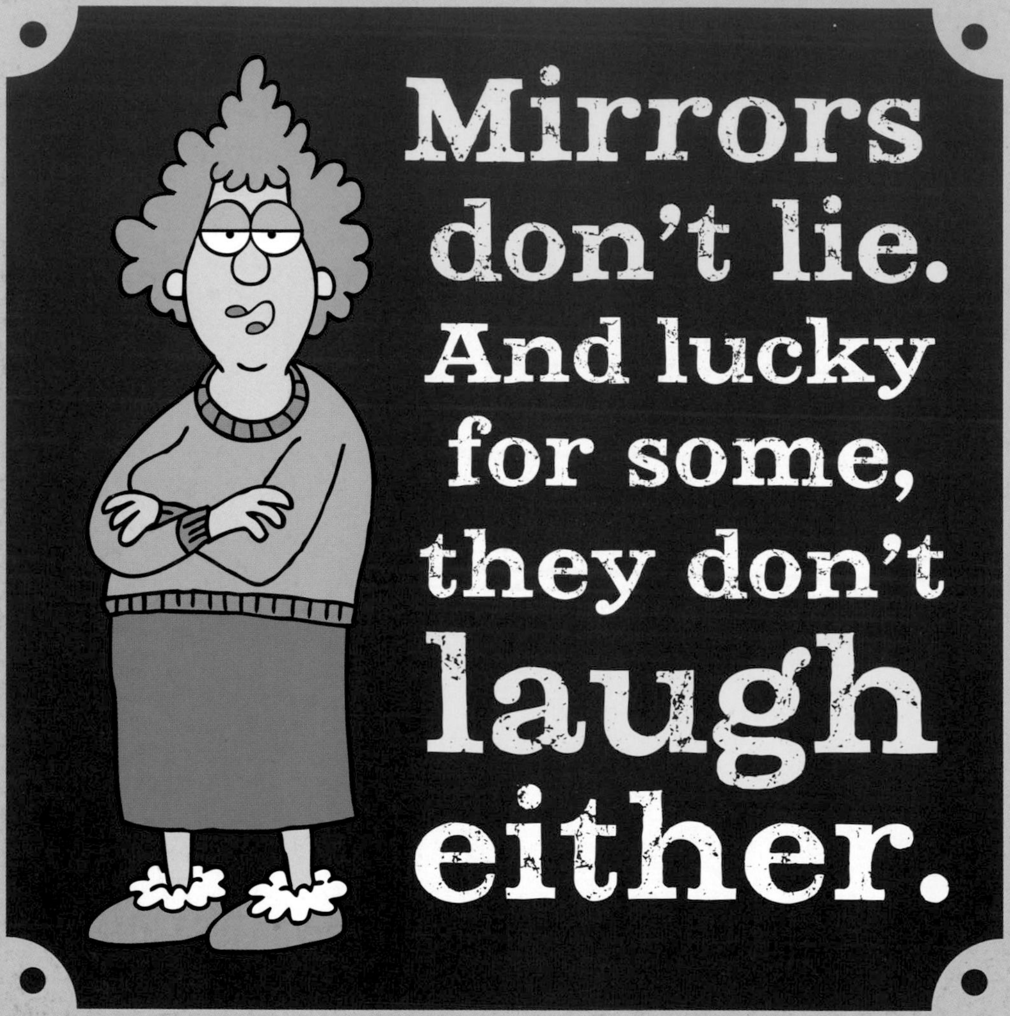
Mirrors don't lie. And lucky for some, they don't laugh either.

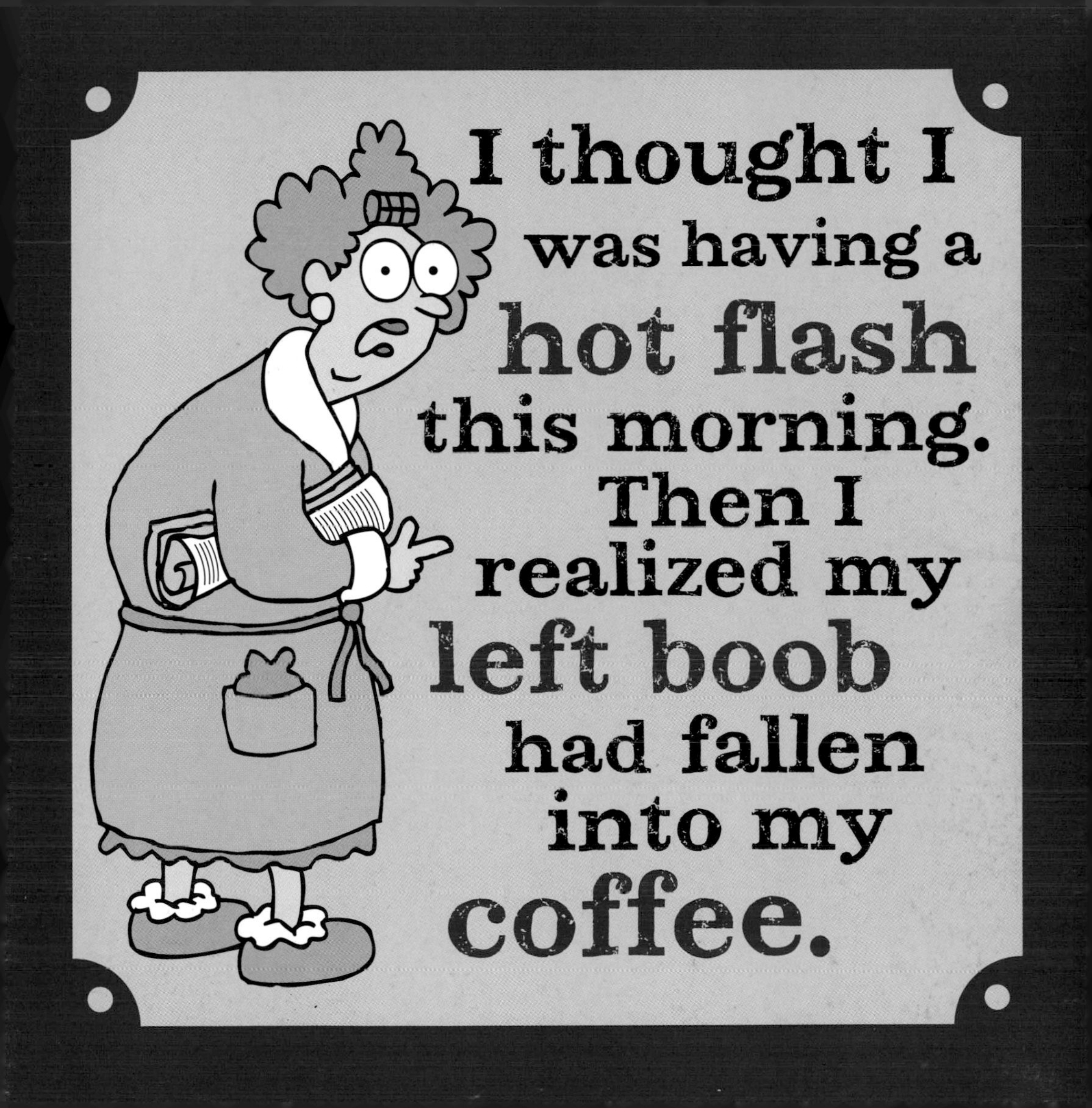

I thought I was having a **hot flash** this morning. Then I realized my **left boob** had fallen into my **coffee.**

Sometimes I wrestle with my **inner** demons.

Other times, we just hug and dance.

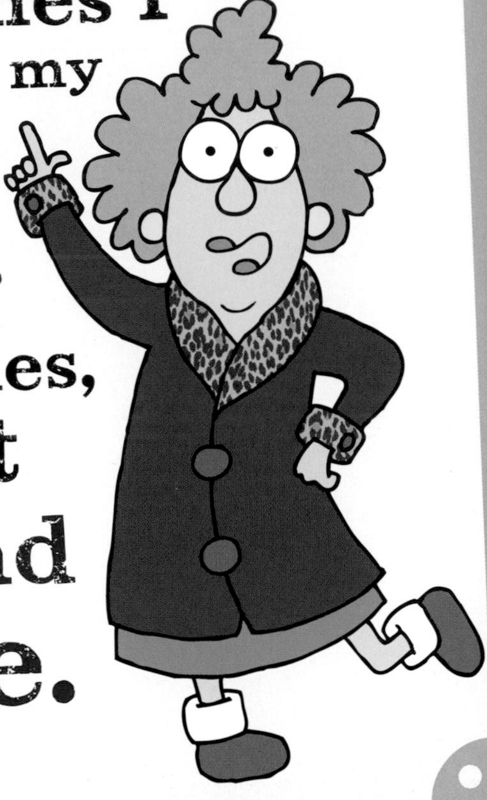

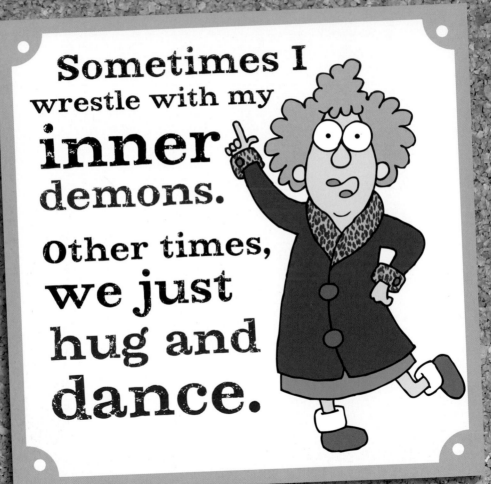

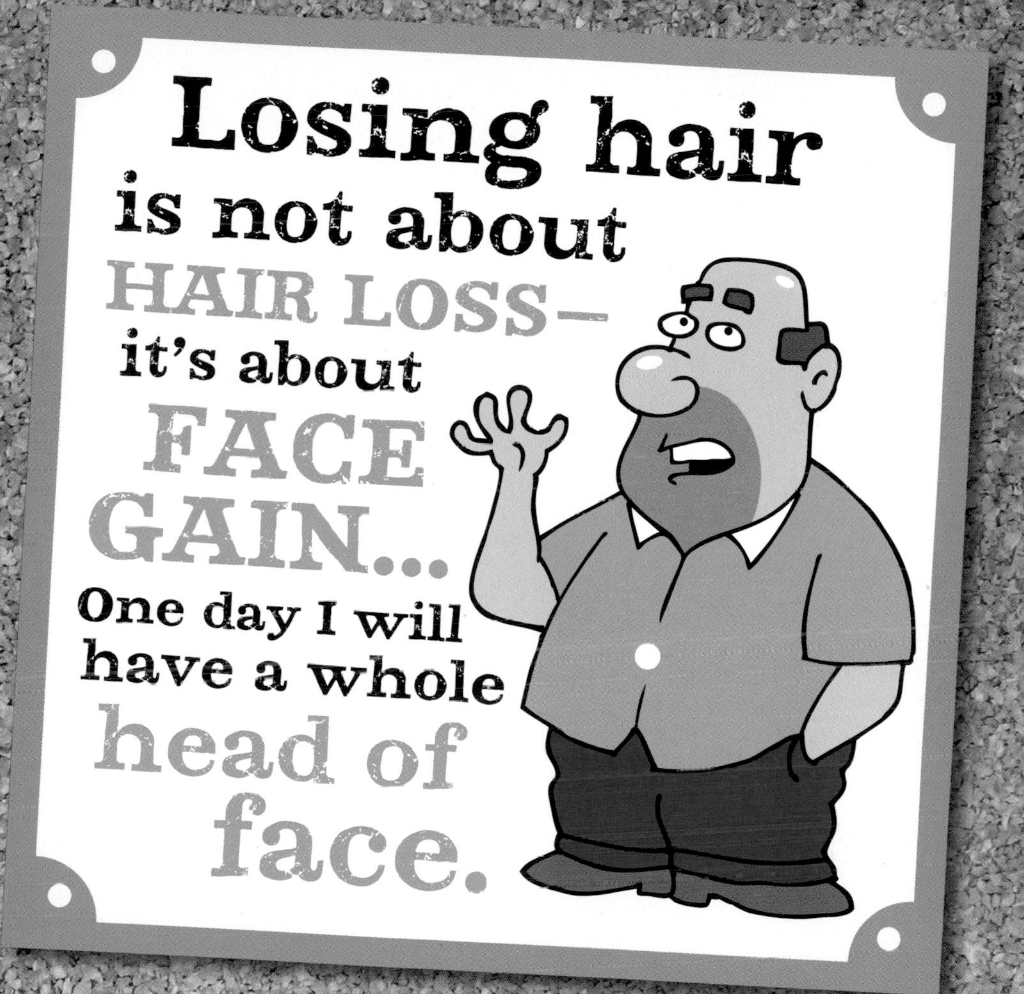
Losing hair
is not about
HAIR LOSS–
it's about
FACE
GAIN...
One day I will
have a whole
head of
face.

AUNTY ACID'S PICK-UP LINES FOR SENIORS No.63

"Hey, good-lookin', you'd better call the paramedics... because I've fallen for you – and I can't get back up."

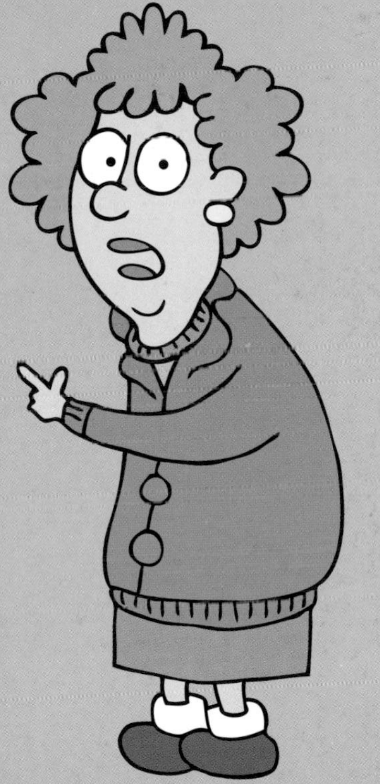

I am proud to announce that I have now reached the age where my driving genuinely terrifies people.

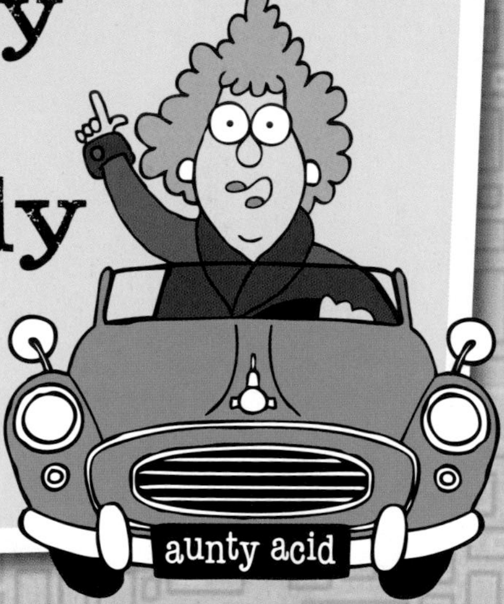

IF AGE HAS TAUGHT ME ONE THING, IT'S THAT YOUNG PEOPLE ARE DUMB!

I know a song, it's called "If you're happy and you know it let Grandma sleep." It's true that the only time I really love talking to children is when I ask them what they want to be when they grow up... because I'm still looking for freakin' ideas!

I've got so many regrets that sometimes I wish I could go back in time and punch myself in the face, but then again I've still got so much to do that I'm just going back to bed instead! Grab yourself a cup of Joe and join me for the following pages that will jiggle your belly with laughter, flap your bingo wings in mirth, and wobble your boobs with giggles.

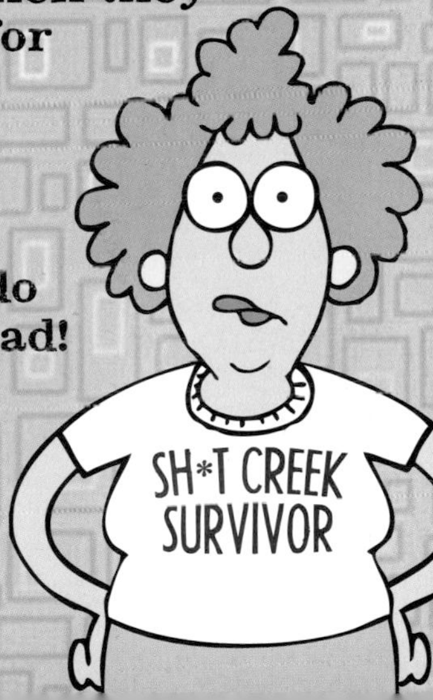
SH*T CREEK
SURVIVOR

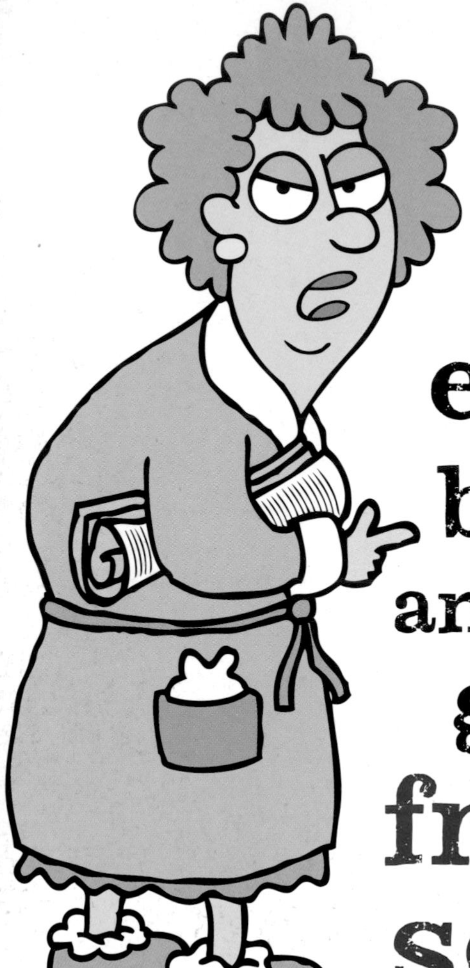

I'm up
—if you're
expecting
bright-eyed
and bushy-tailed
go catch a
freakin'
squirrel.

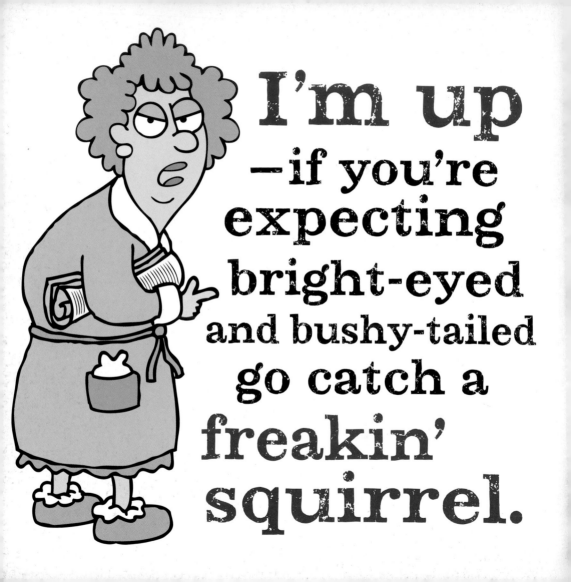

I can
rise and shine,
but not
at the
same
time.

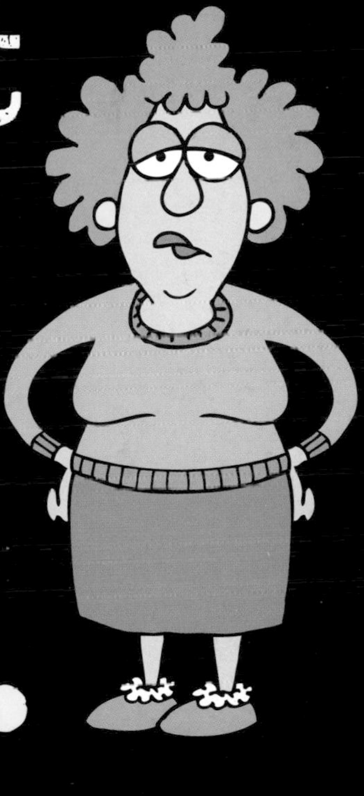

Me and Walt have been together so long, we finish each other's sentences. Usually with the words, "Shut the Hell up!"

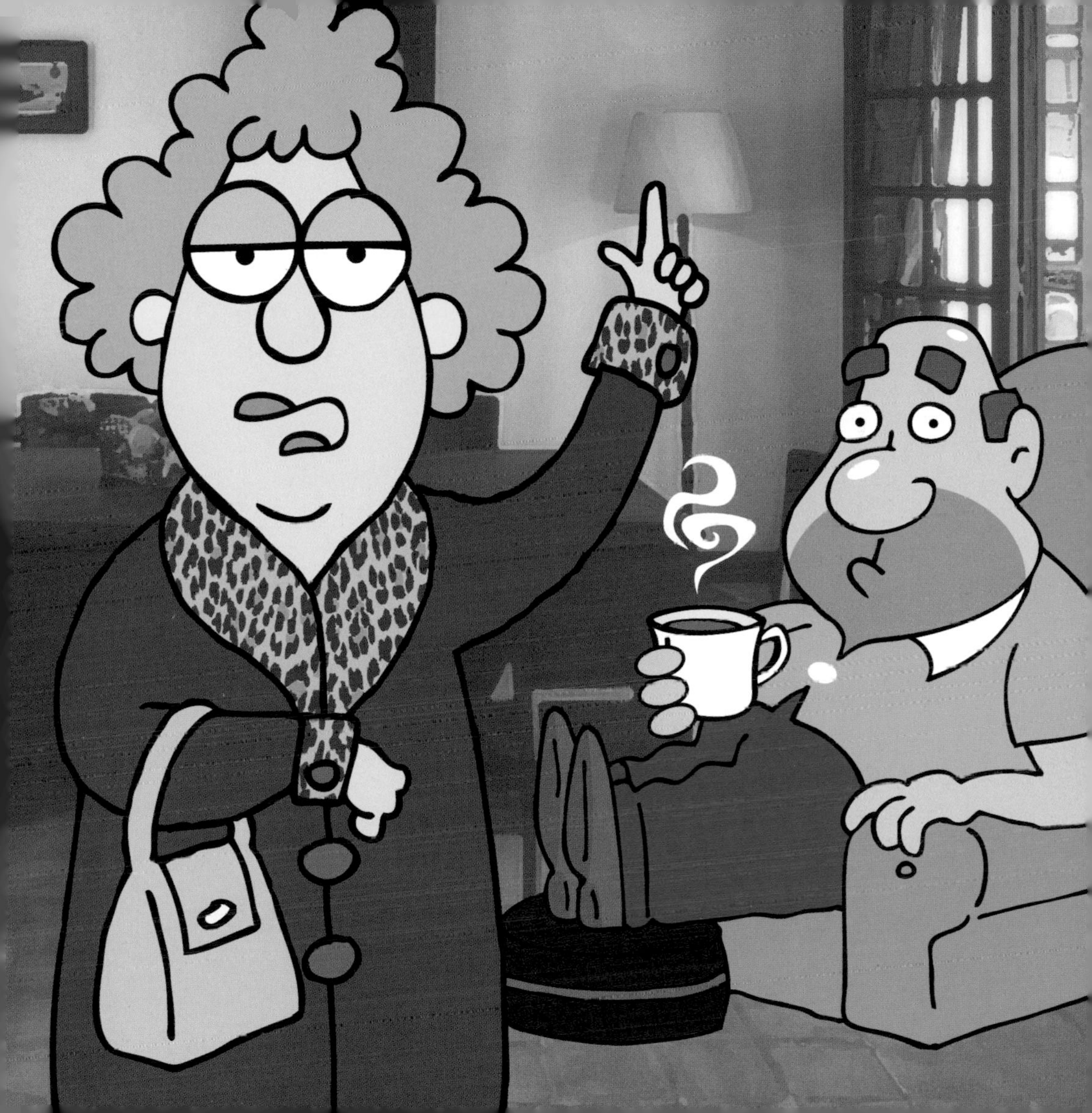

When I woke up this morning... No wrinkles in sight. The house was spotless. The garden looked lovely. And my grumpy bloke looked like George Clooney. I don't think I'll ever put my glasses on again.

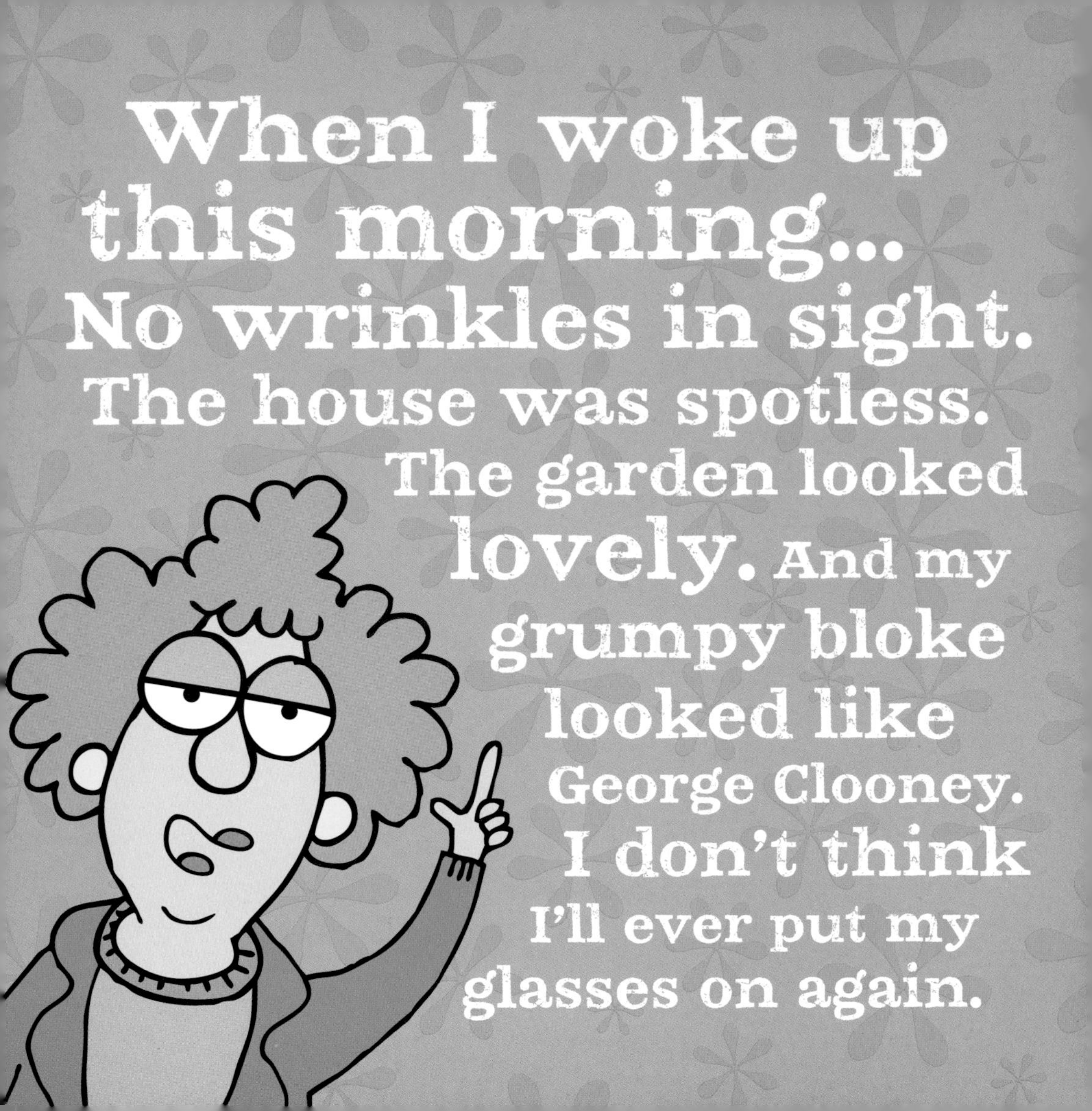

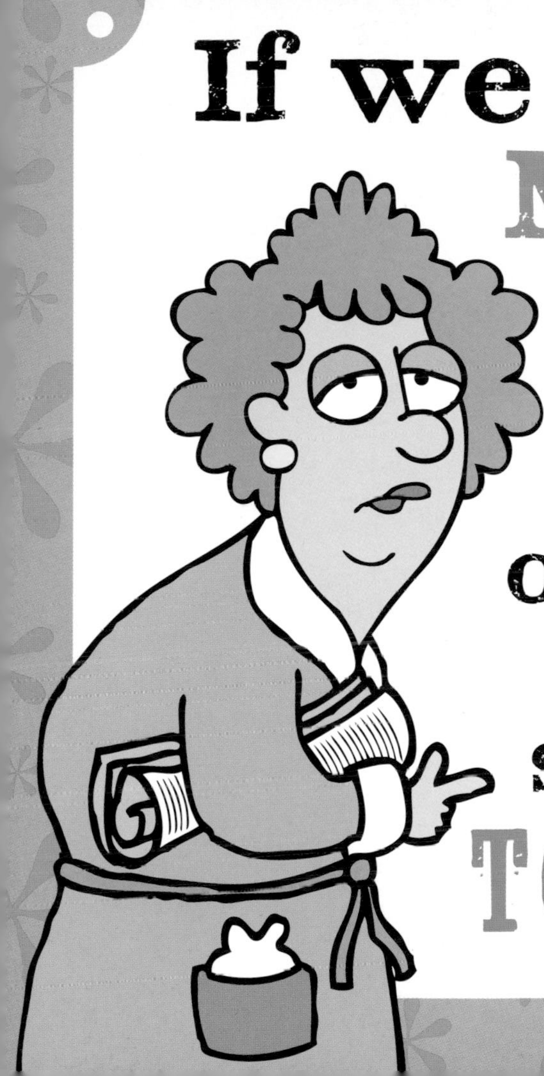

If we were MEANT to "POP" out of bed, we'd all sleep in TOASTERS.

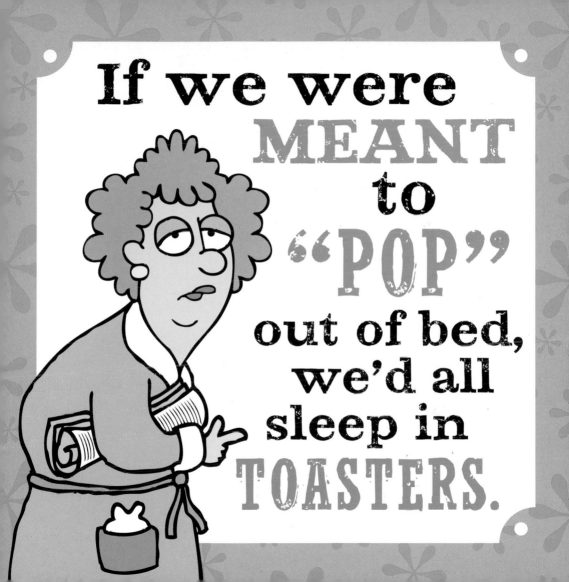

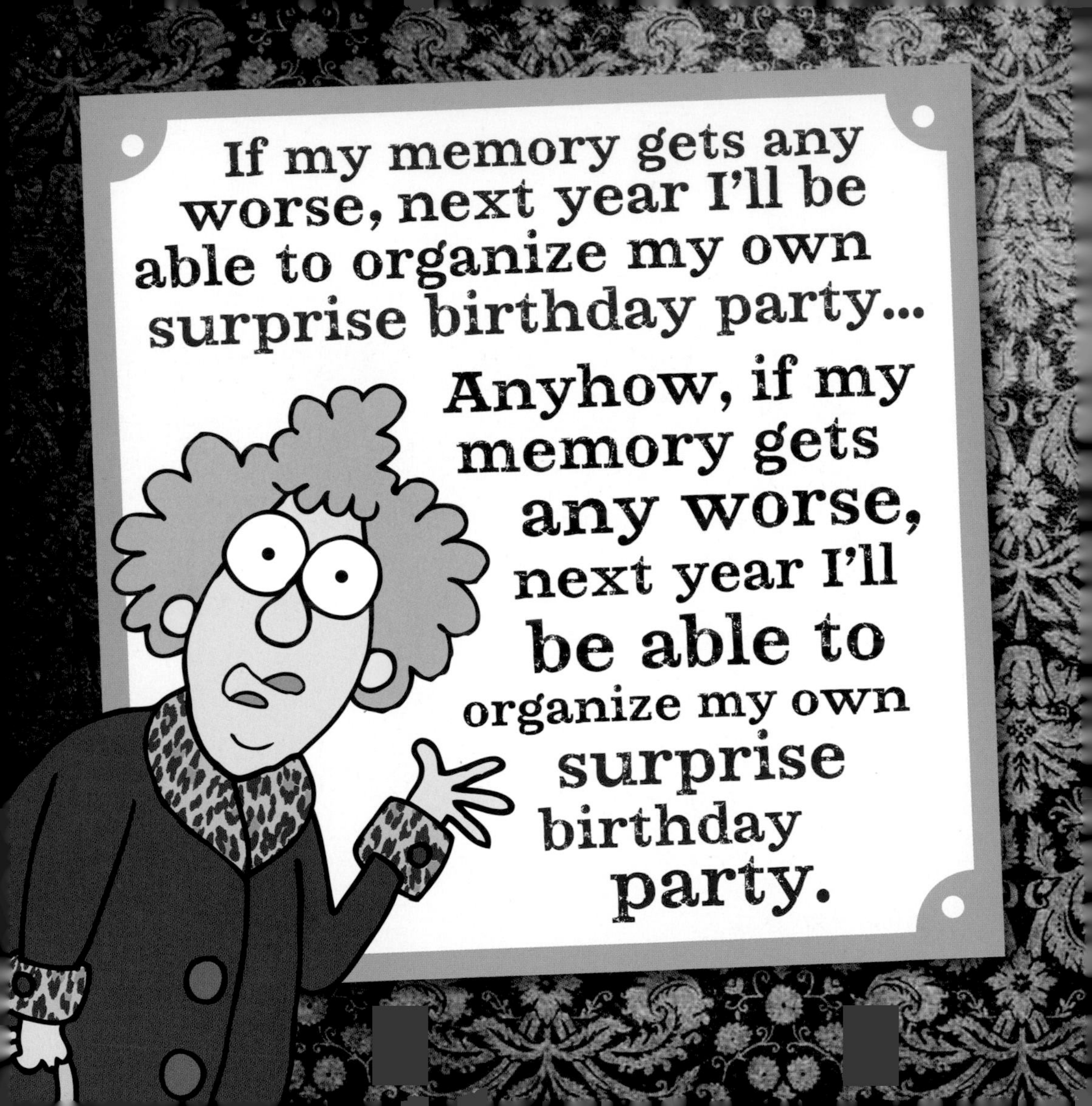
If my memory gets any worse, next year I'll be able to organize my own surprise birthday party...
Anyhow, if my memory gets any worse, next year I'll be able to organize my own surprise birthday party.

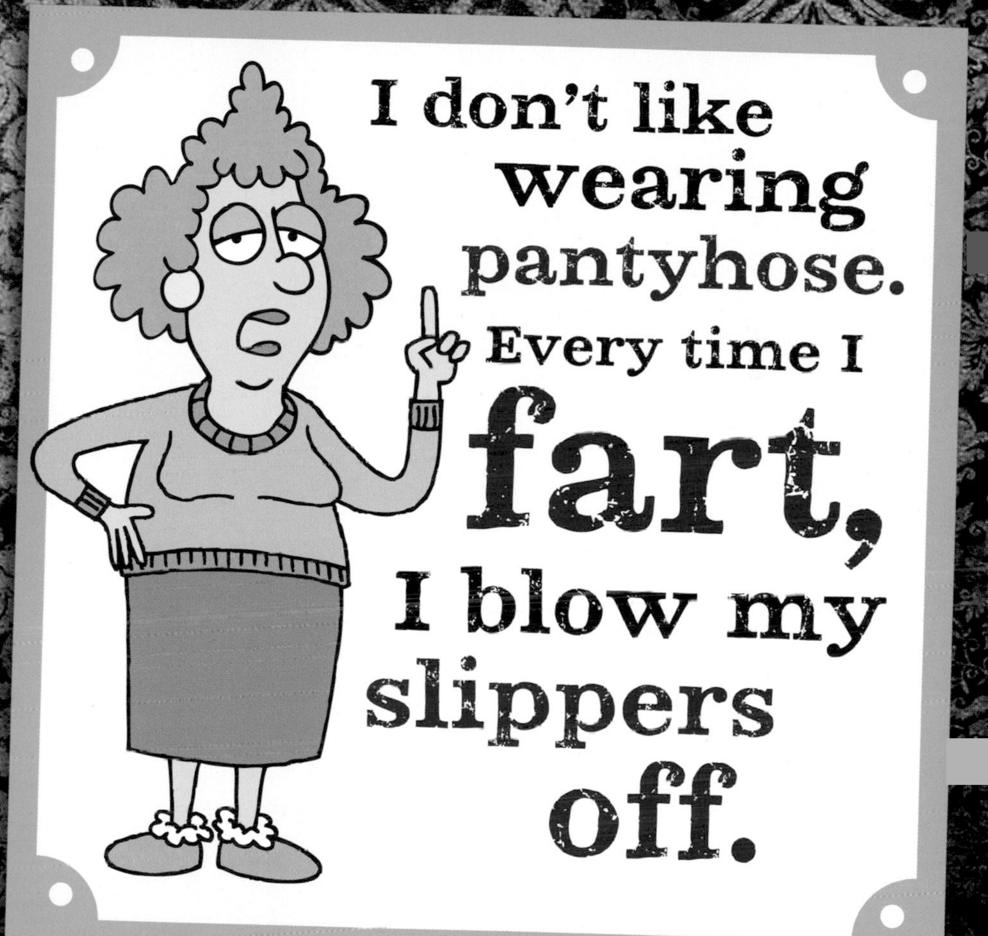
I don't like
wearing
pantyhose.
Every time I
fart,
I blow my
slippers
off.

LIFE is SHORT.
Smile while you still have TEETH.

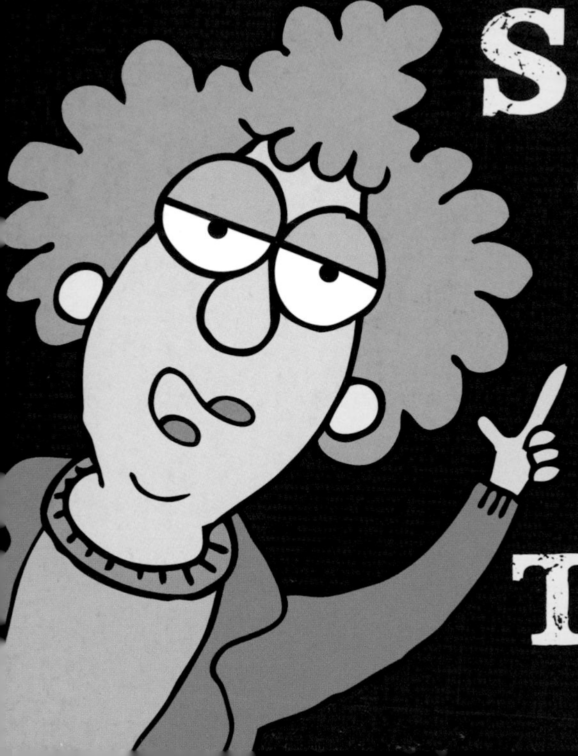

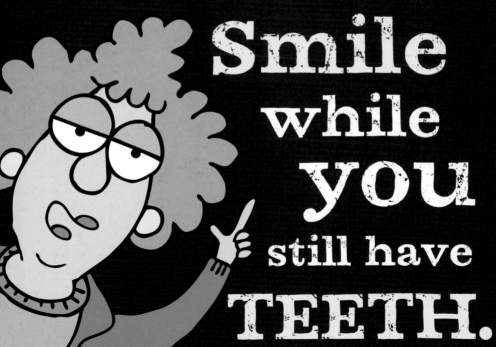

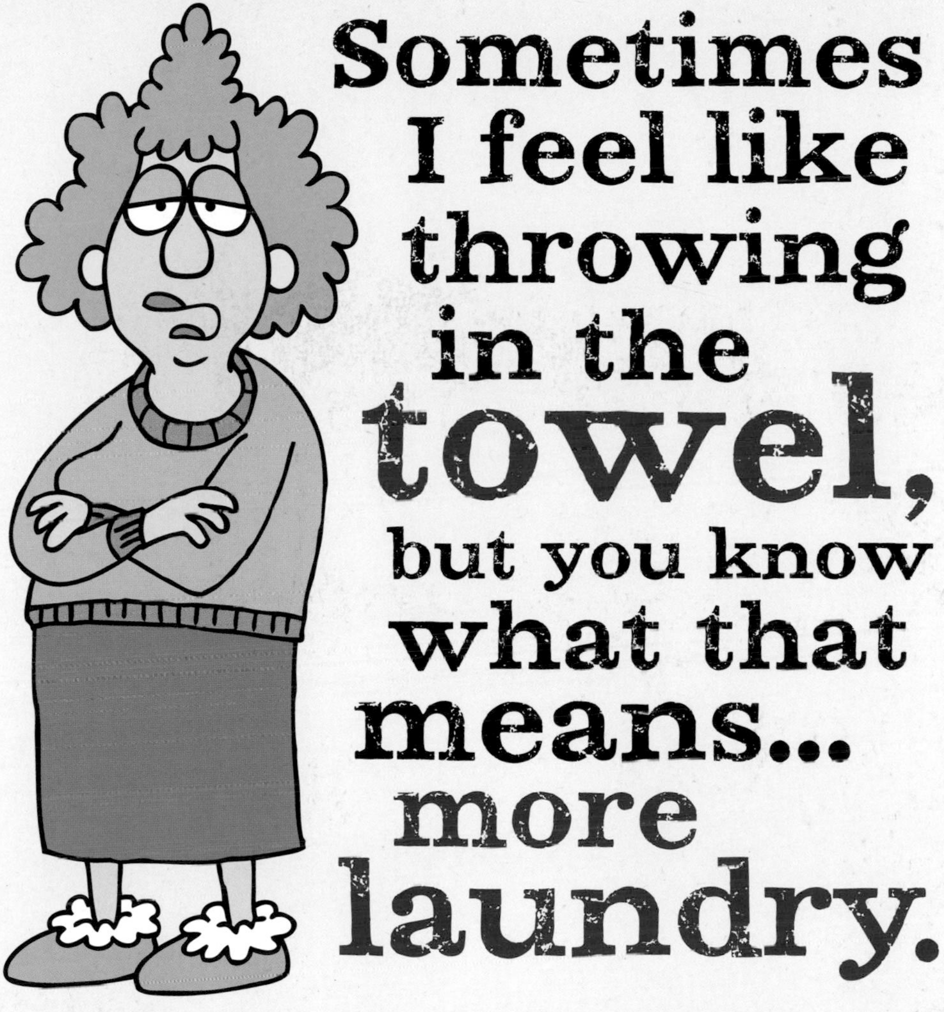

Sometimes
I feel like
throwing
in the
towel,
but you know
what that
means...
more
laundry.

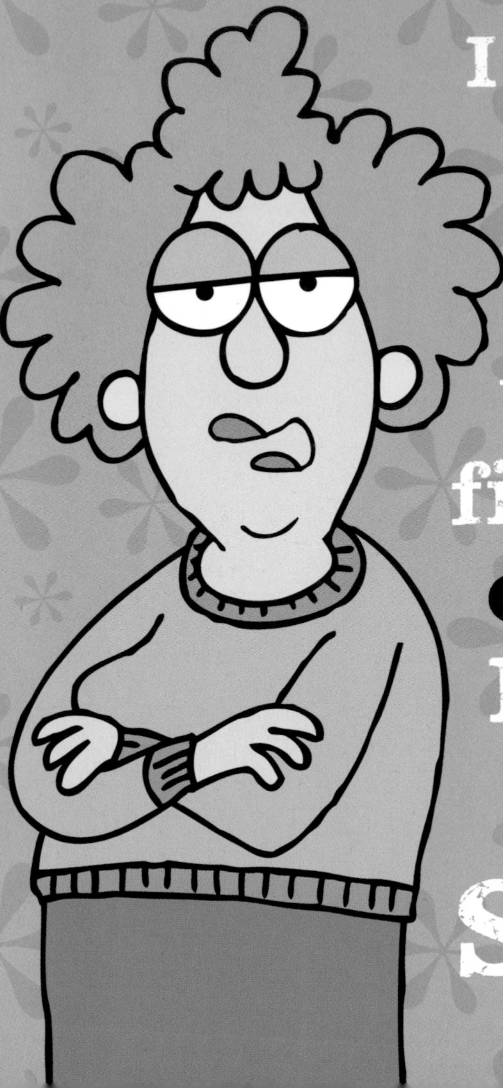

I don't want to make anyone **jealous,** but I can still fit into the **earrings** I wore in High School.

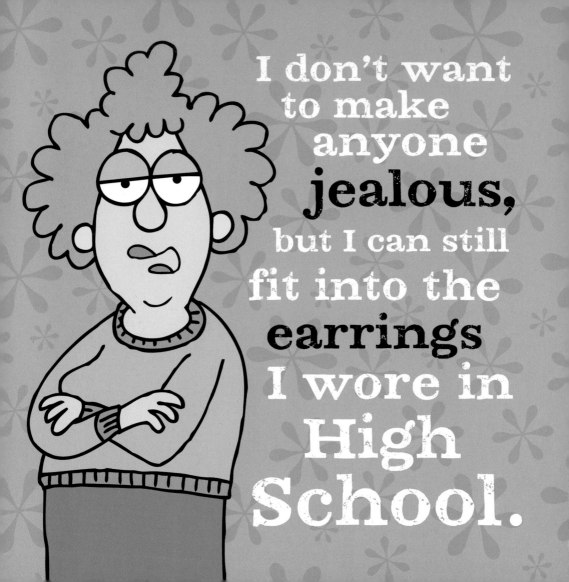

I'm EXHAUSTIPATED, which means I'm just too tired to give a crap!

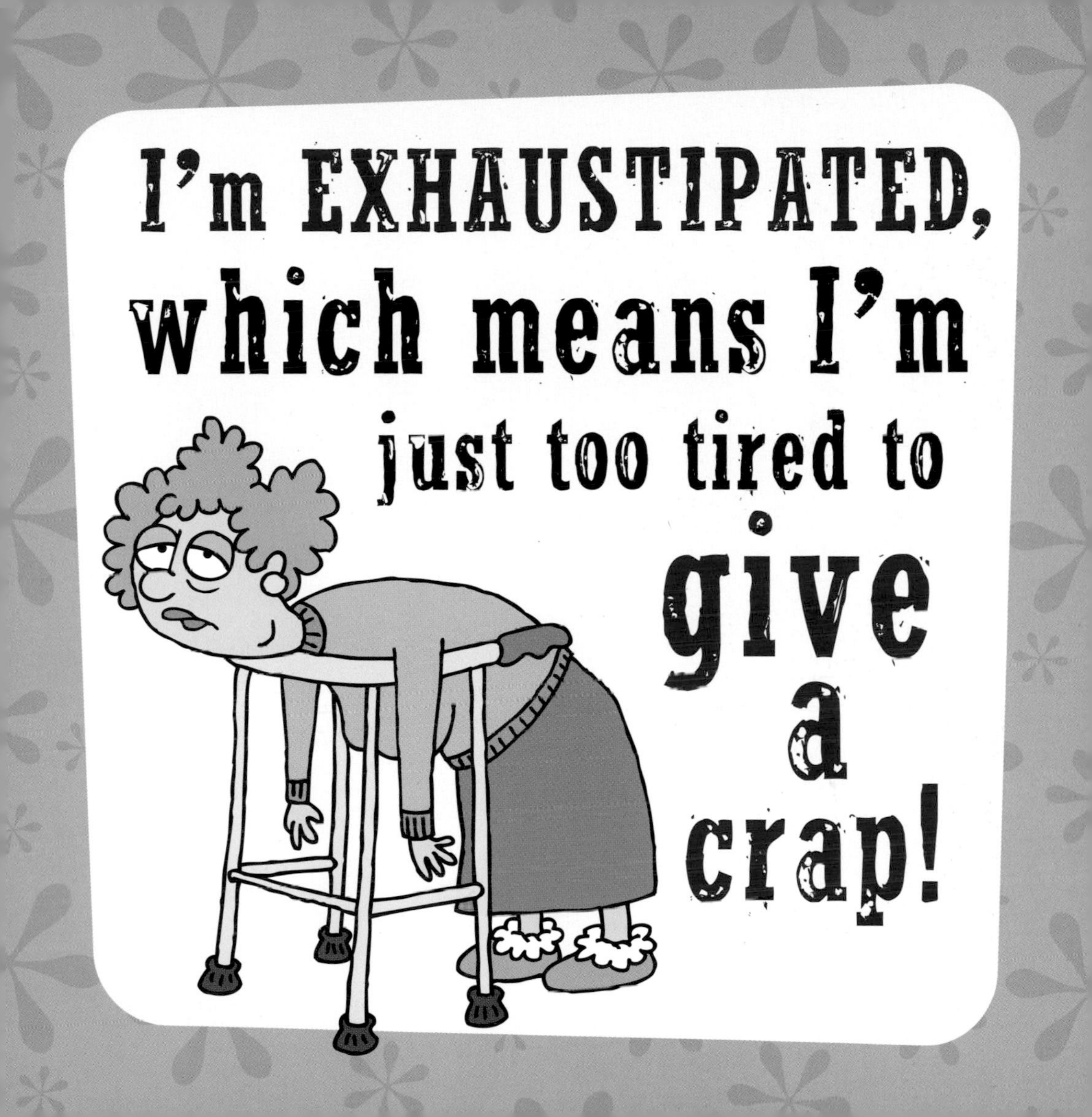

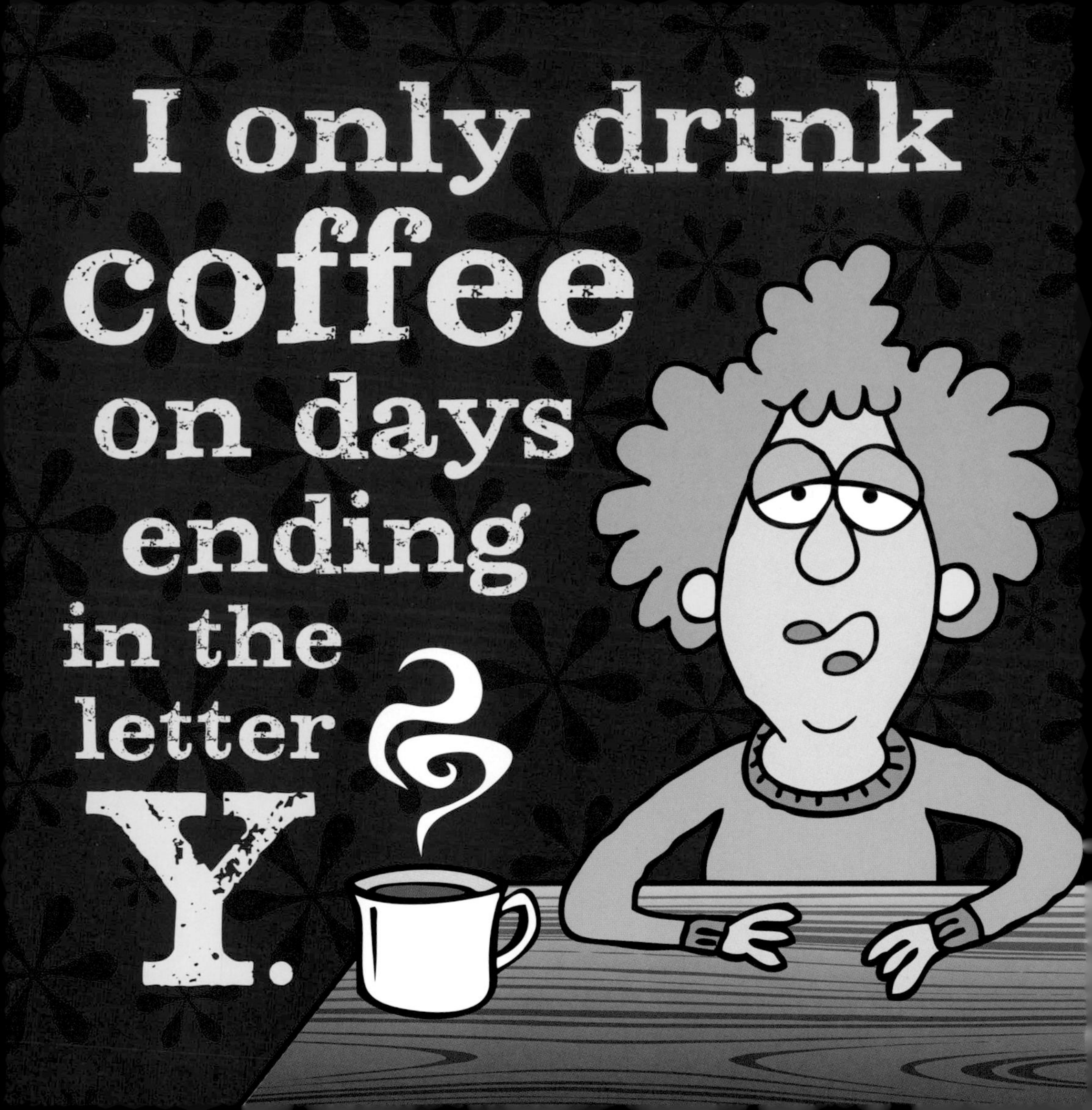
I only drink
coffee
on days
ending
in the
letter
Y.

If
life's a journey,
mine is
between
the fridge
and the
computer.

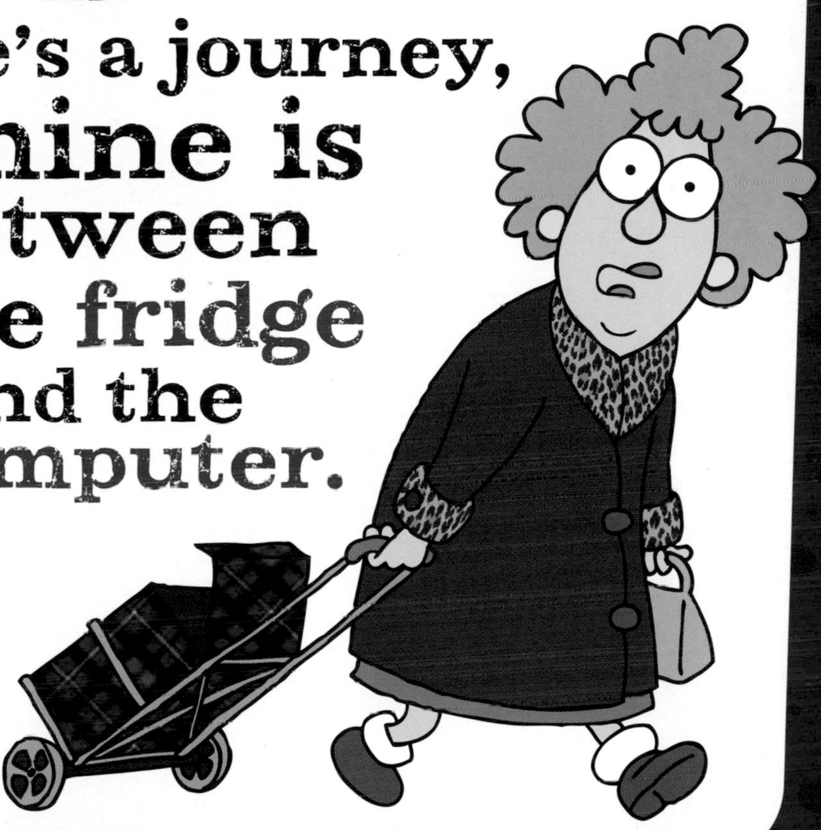

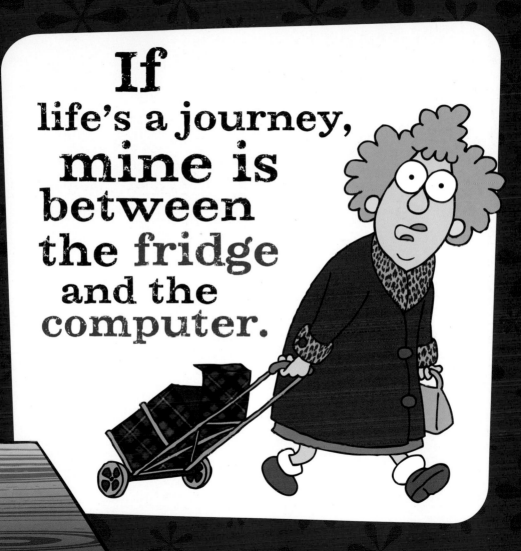

My favorite outdoor activity is going back inside.

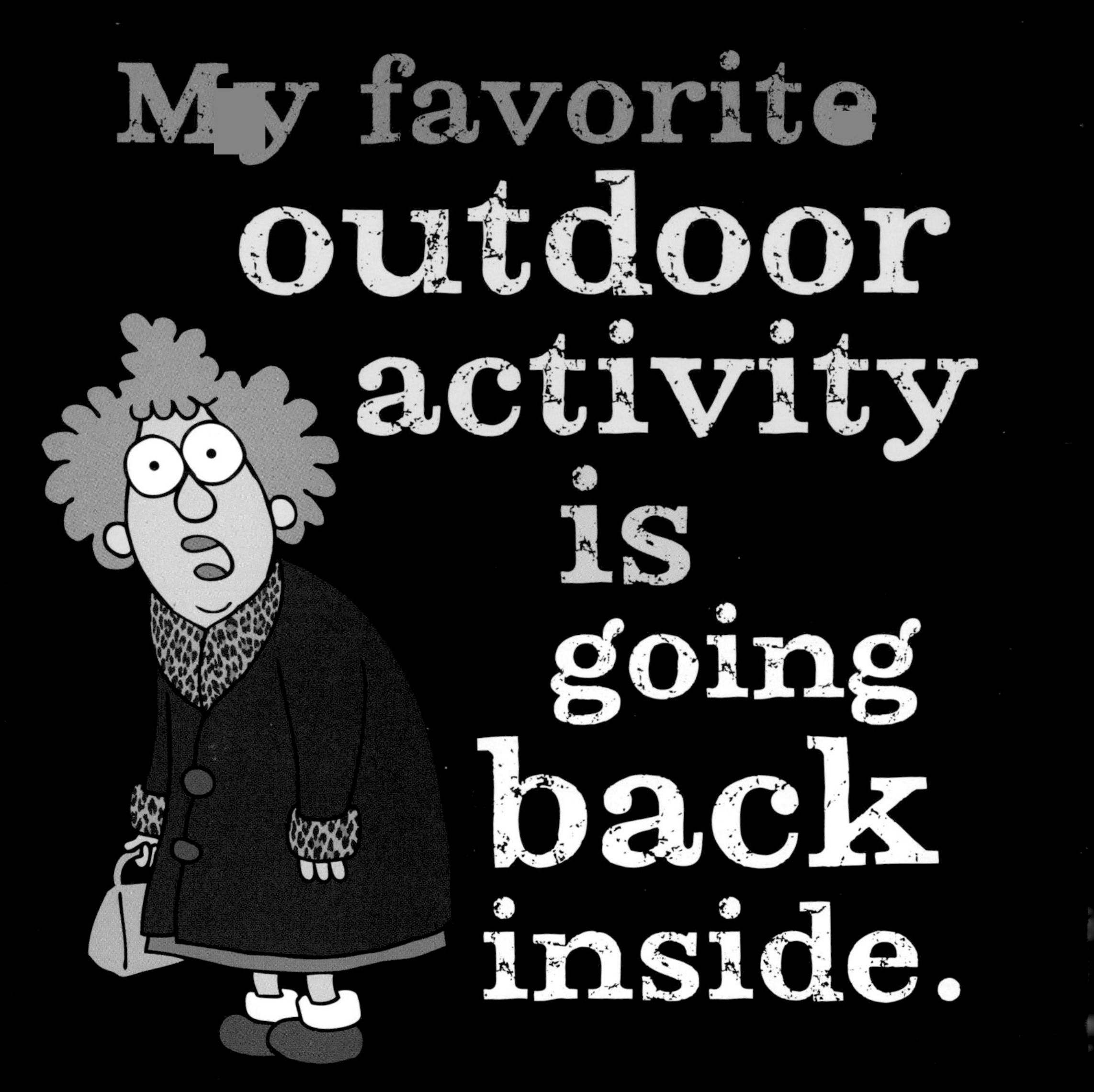

I remember the words to every song from the '80s...
But forget why I walked into a room.

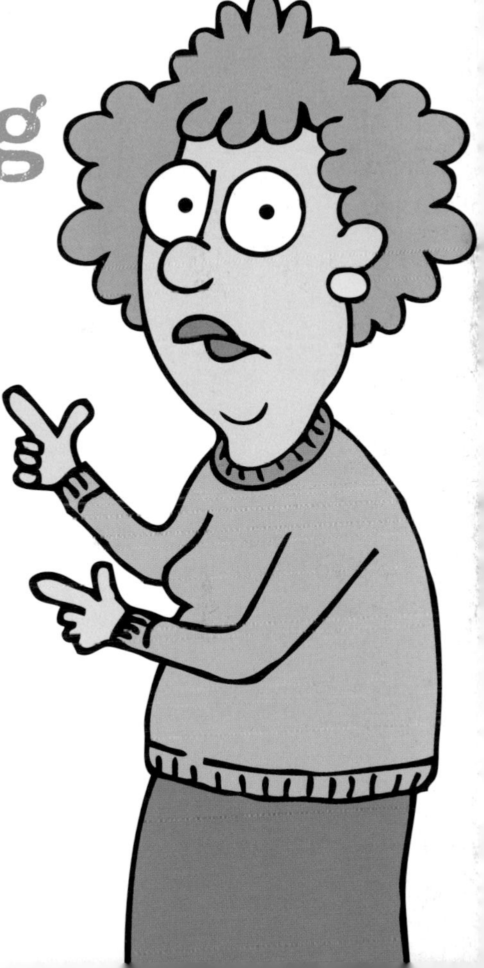

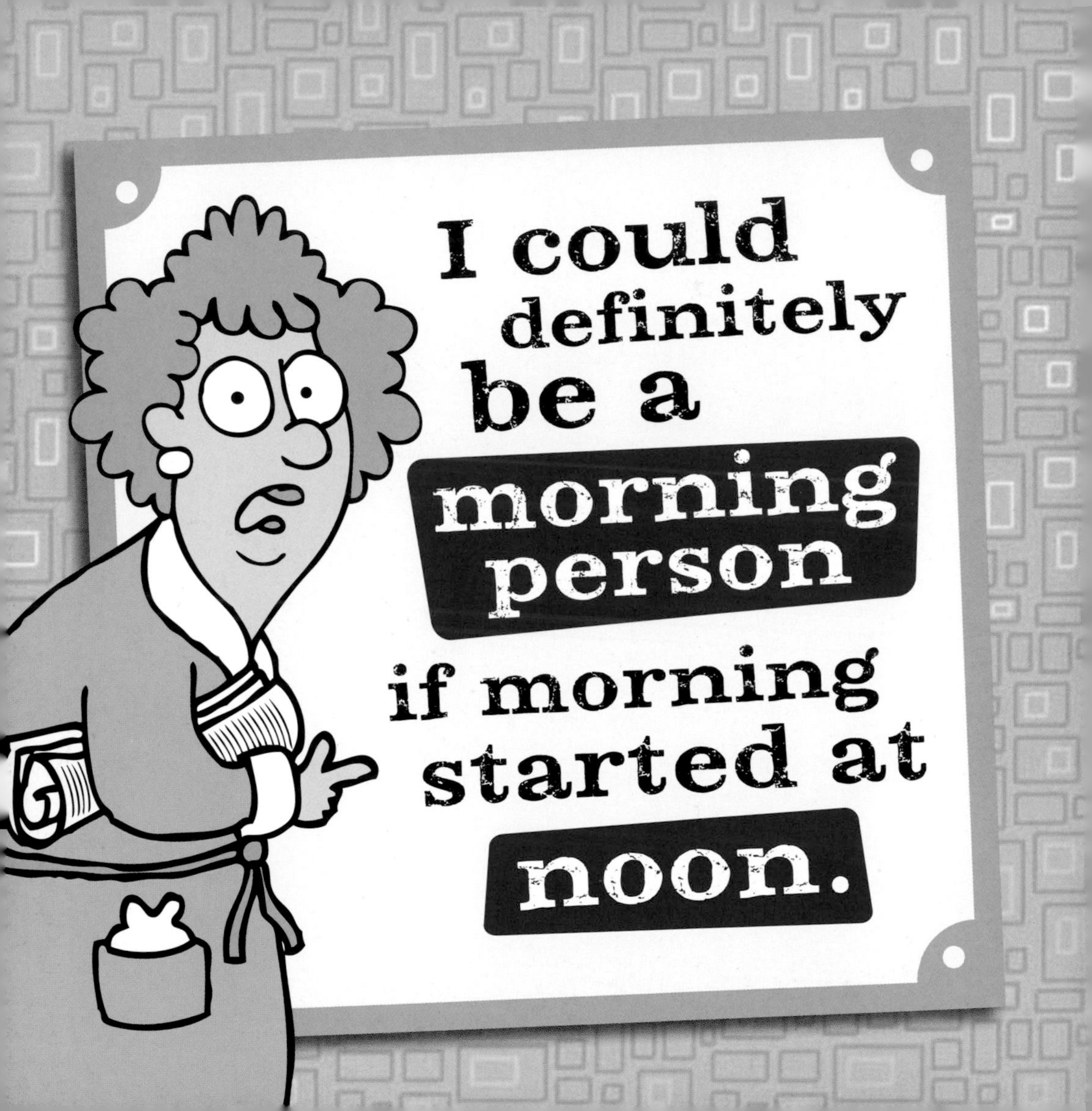
I could
definitely
be a
morning
person
if morning
started at
noon.

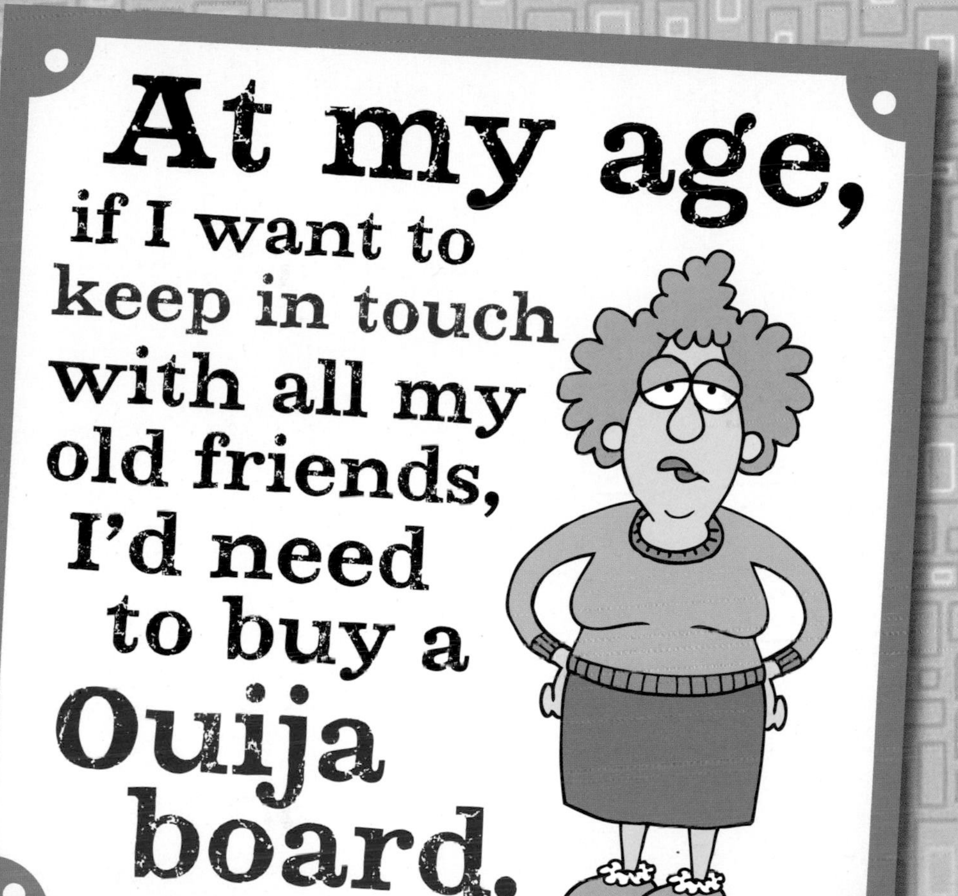
At my age,
if I want to
keep in touch
with all my
old friends,
I'd need
to buy a
Ouija
board.

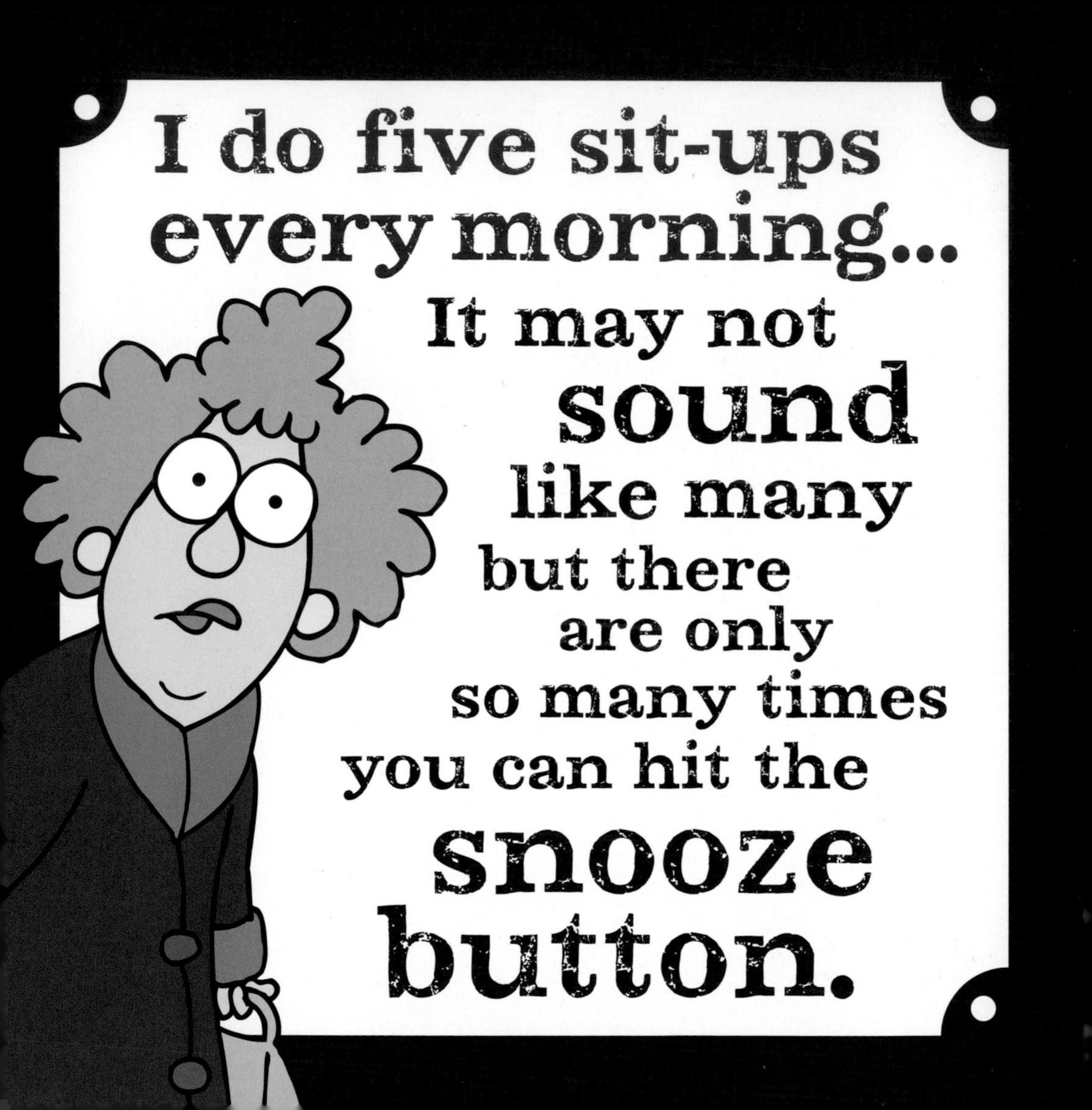

I do five sit-ups every morning...
It may not **sound** like many but there are only so many times you can hit the **snooze button.**

I'm so old I can LAUGH COUGH SNEEZE & PEE all at the same time.

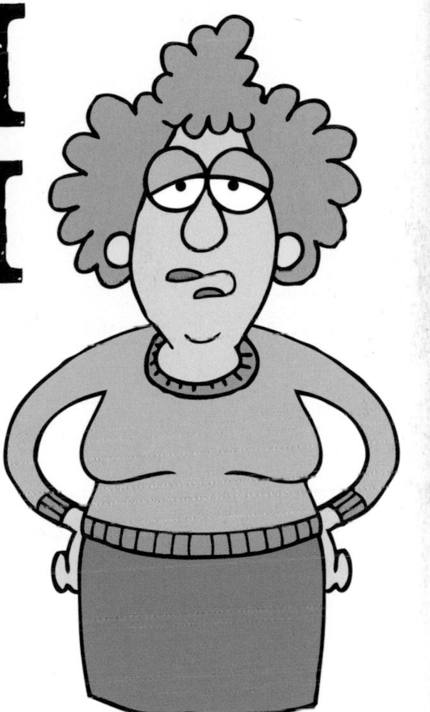

There comes a time in life **when you should stop** bending over backwards for people **and start** leaning forwards— **so they can** kiss your ass.

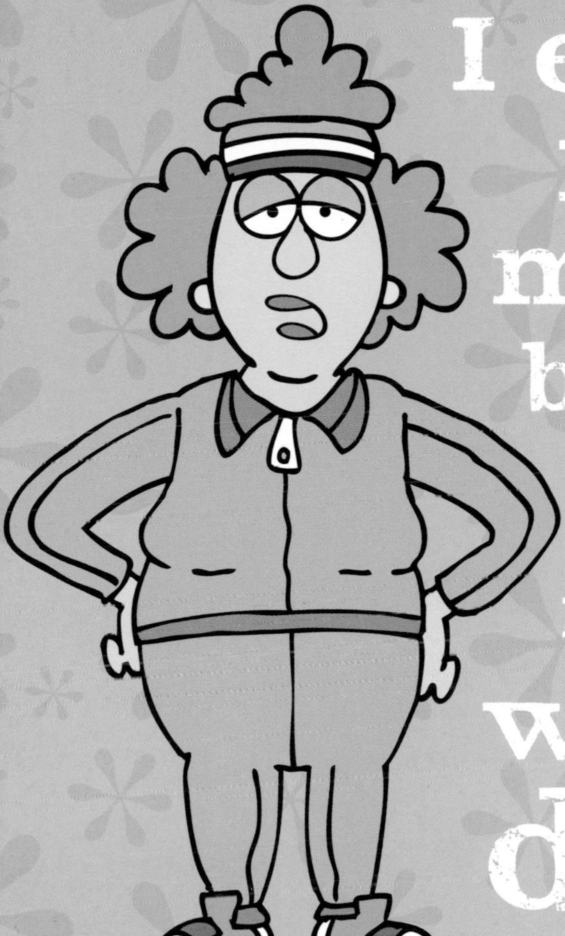

I exercise in the morning, before my **brain** figures out what I'm **doing.**

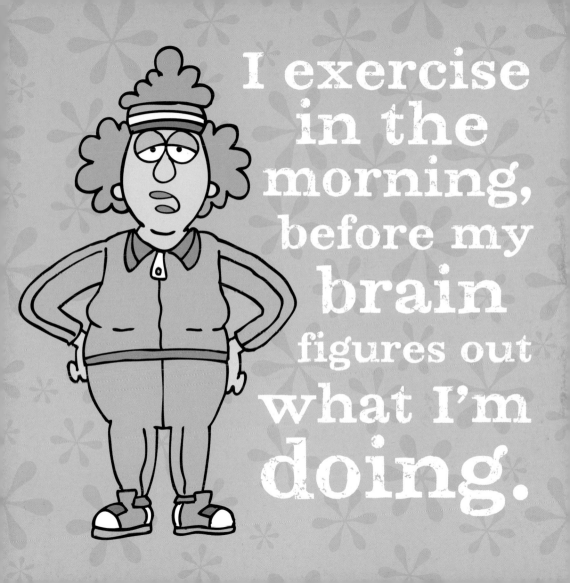

I MARRIED MY HUSBAND FOR HIS LOOKS, BUT NOT THE ONE'S HE'S GIVING ME LATELY!

Walt and I have been married so long sometimes we have to do things to put the spice back into our relationship. He bought some Viagra the other week but all it did was make sure he didn't pee on his shoes.

I didn't feel disappointed though, these days I don't feel anything until noon and then it's time for my nap...

Enjoy the following pages of dating tips for old divas, sex in your sixties, and late loving!

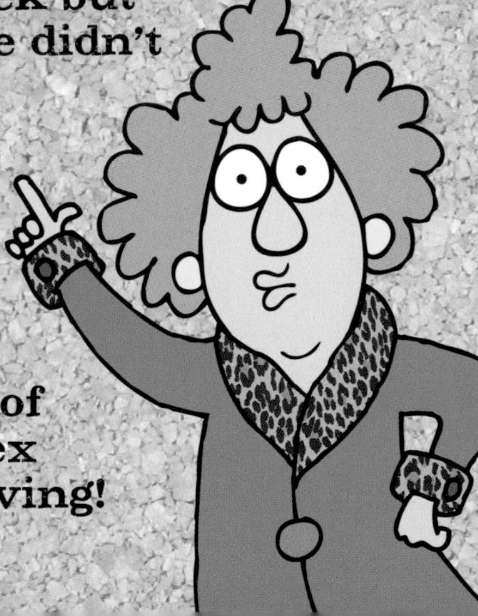

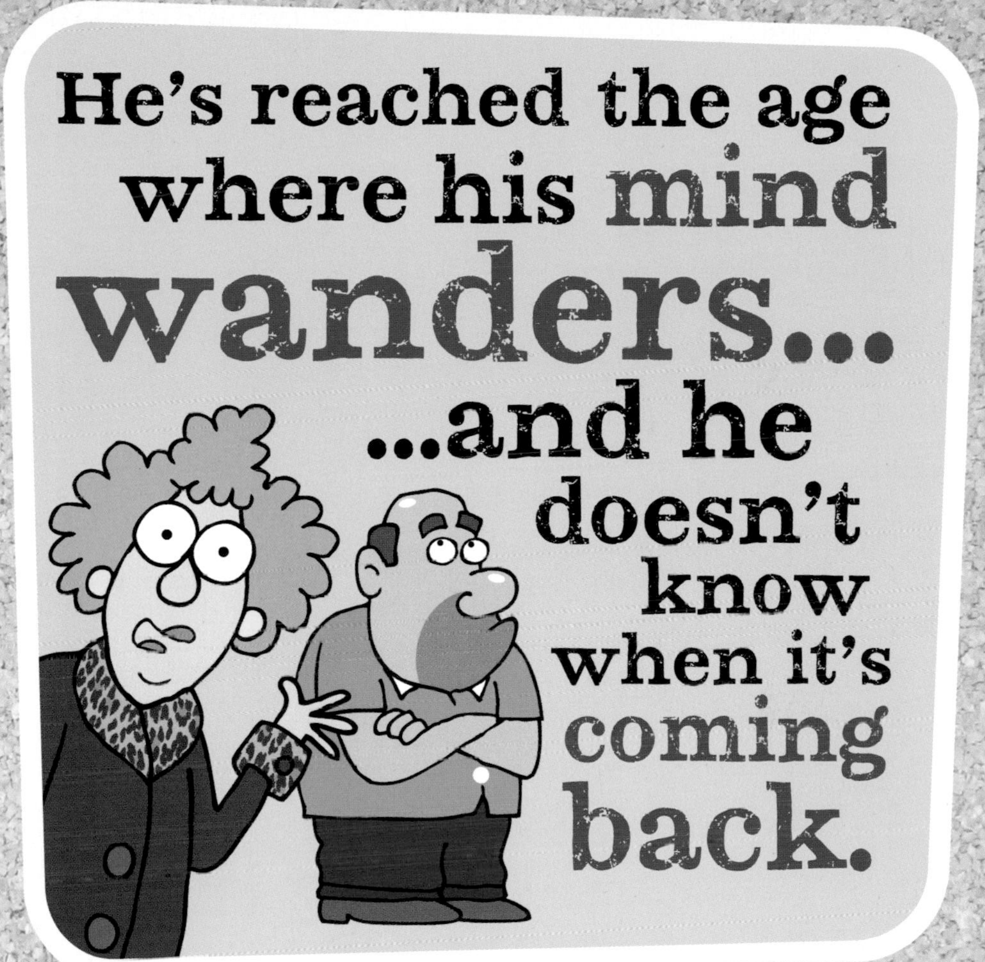
He's reached the age
where his mind
wanders...
...and he
doesn't
know
when it's
coming
back.

Today I feel like **WONDER WOMAN** Because I wonder where I've put my keys, I wonder where I've put my purse and I wonder where all my cash has gone.

I'm the crazy Aunt everybody warns you about.

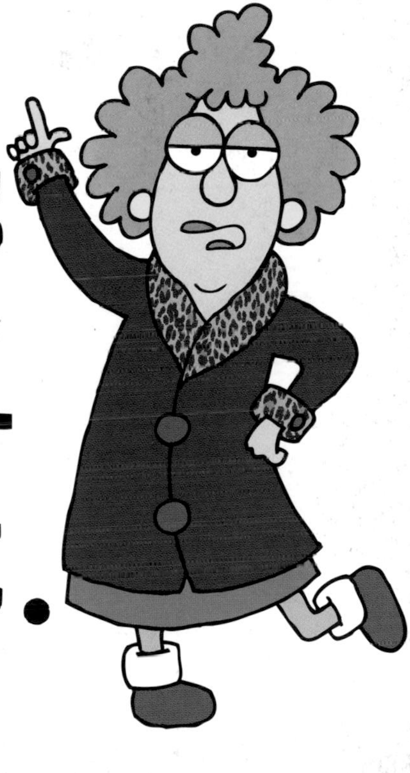

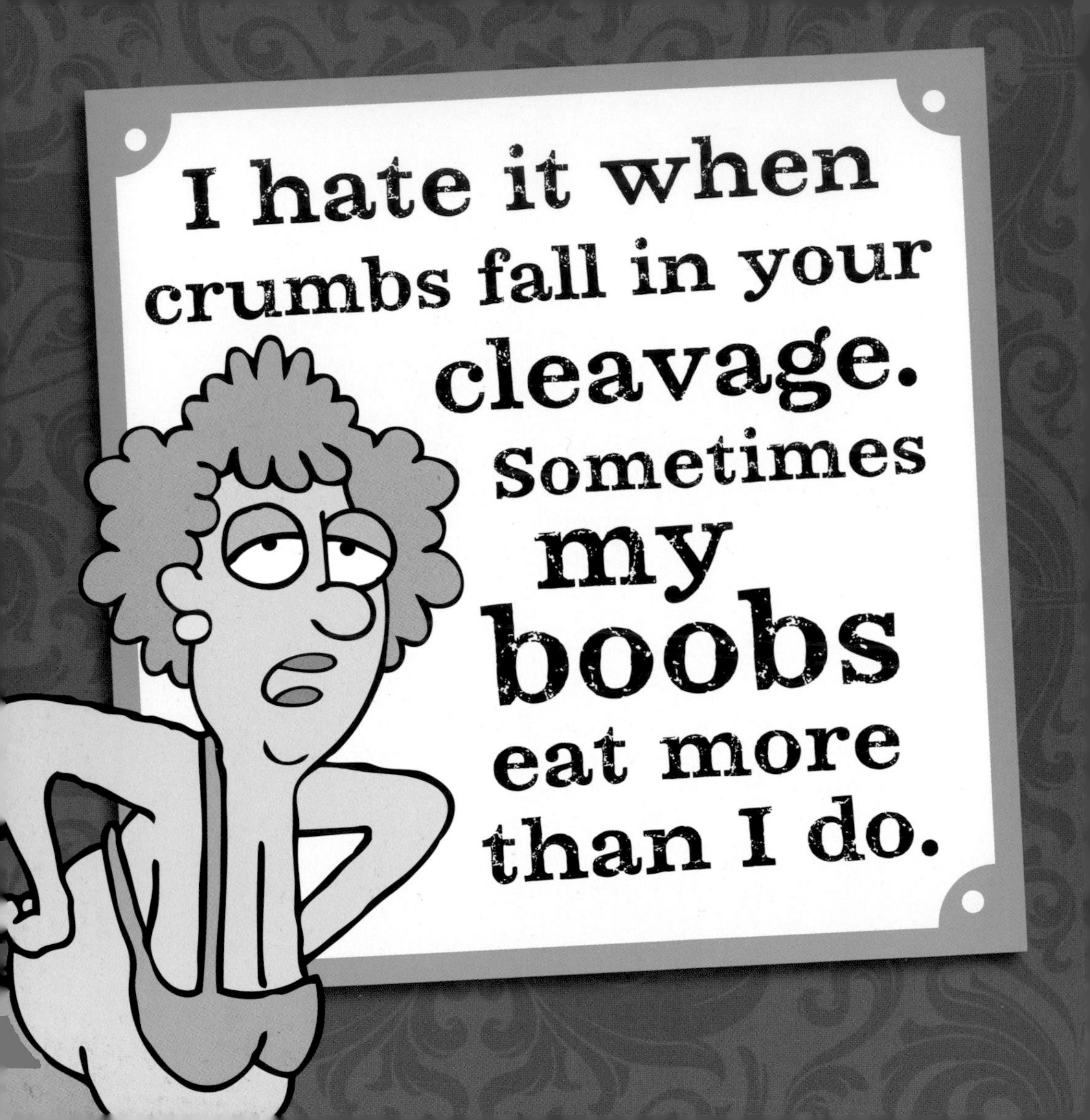
I hate it when crumbs fall in your cleavage. Sometimes my boobs eat more than I do.

I'm getting old...
I got out of bed and had
chest pains...
I looked down
and realized
I was
standing
on my
nipples.

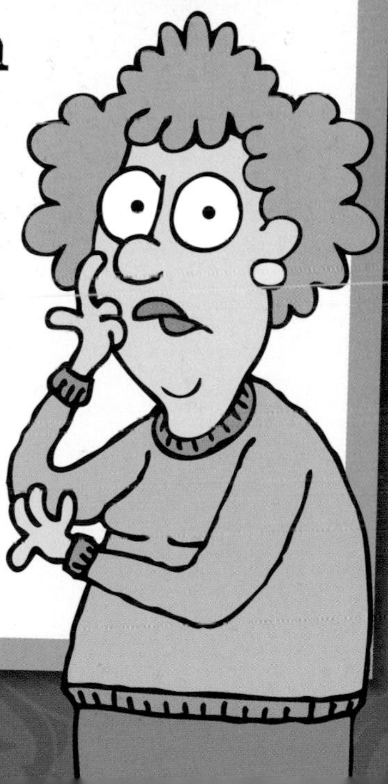

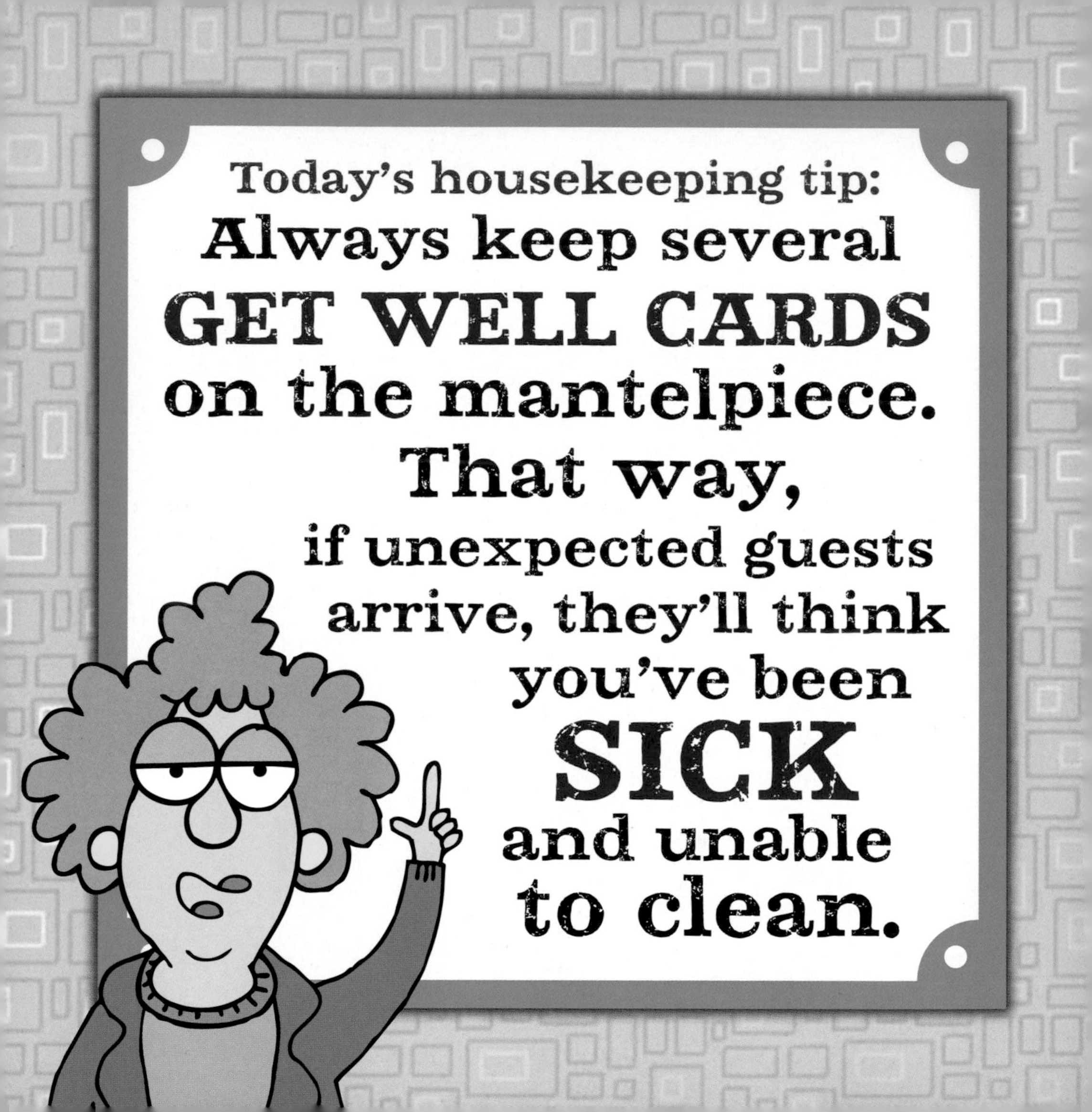
Today's housekeeping tip:
Always keep several
GET WELL CARDS
on the mantelpiece.
That way,
if unexpected guests
arrive, they'll think
you've been
SICK
and unable
to clean.

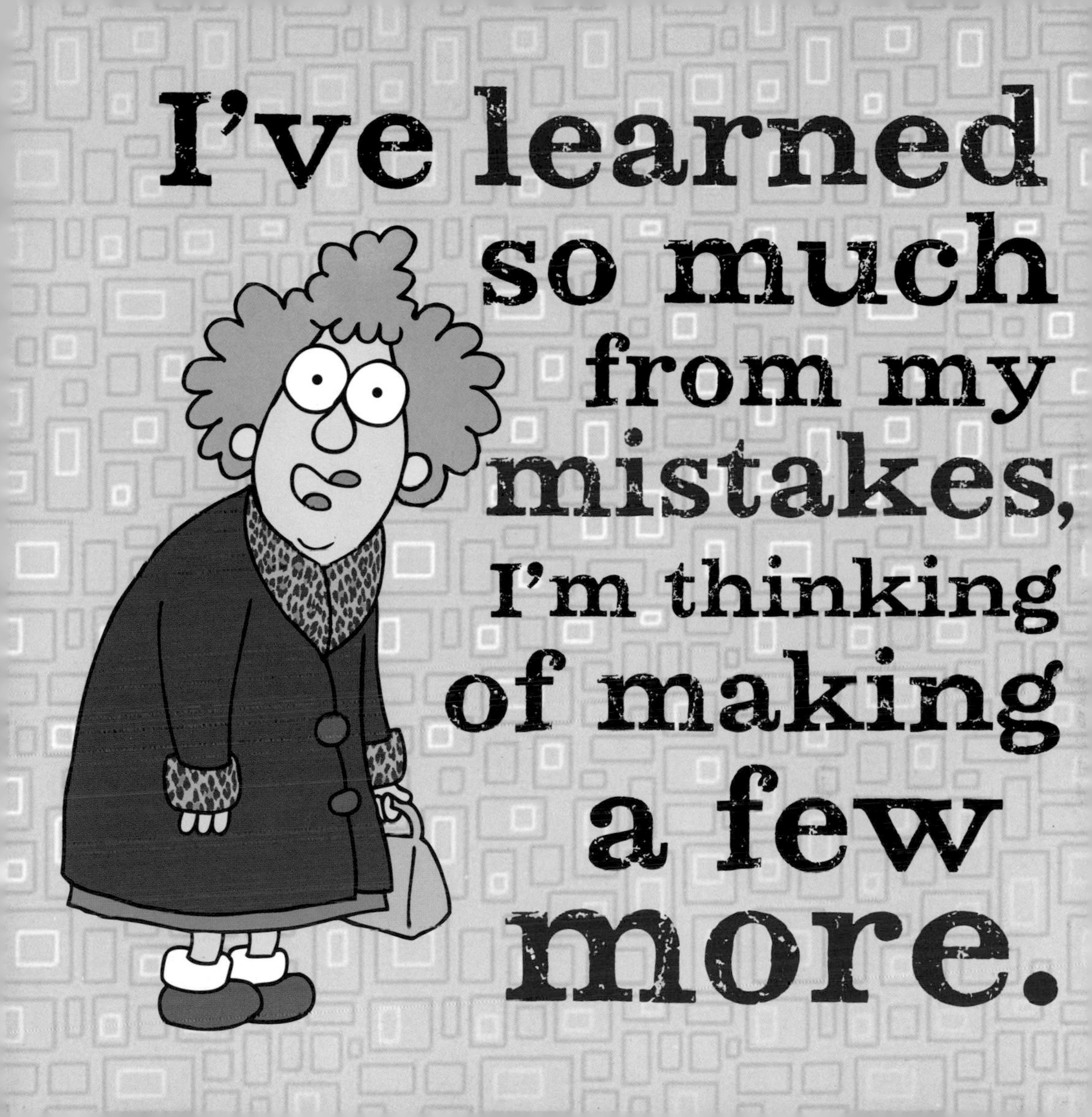
I've learned
so much
from my
mistakes,
I'm thinking
of making
a few
more.

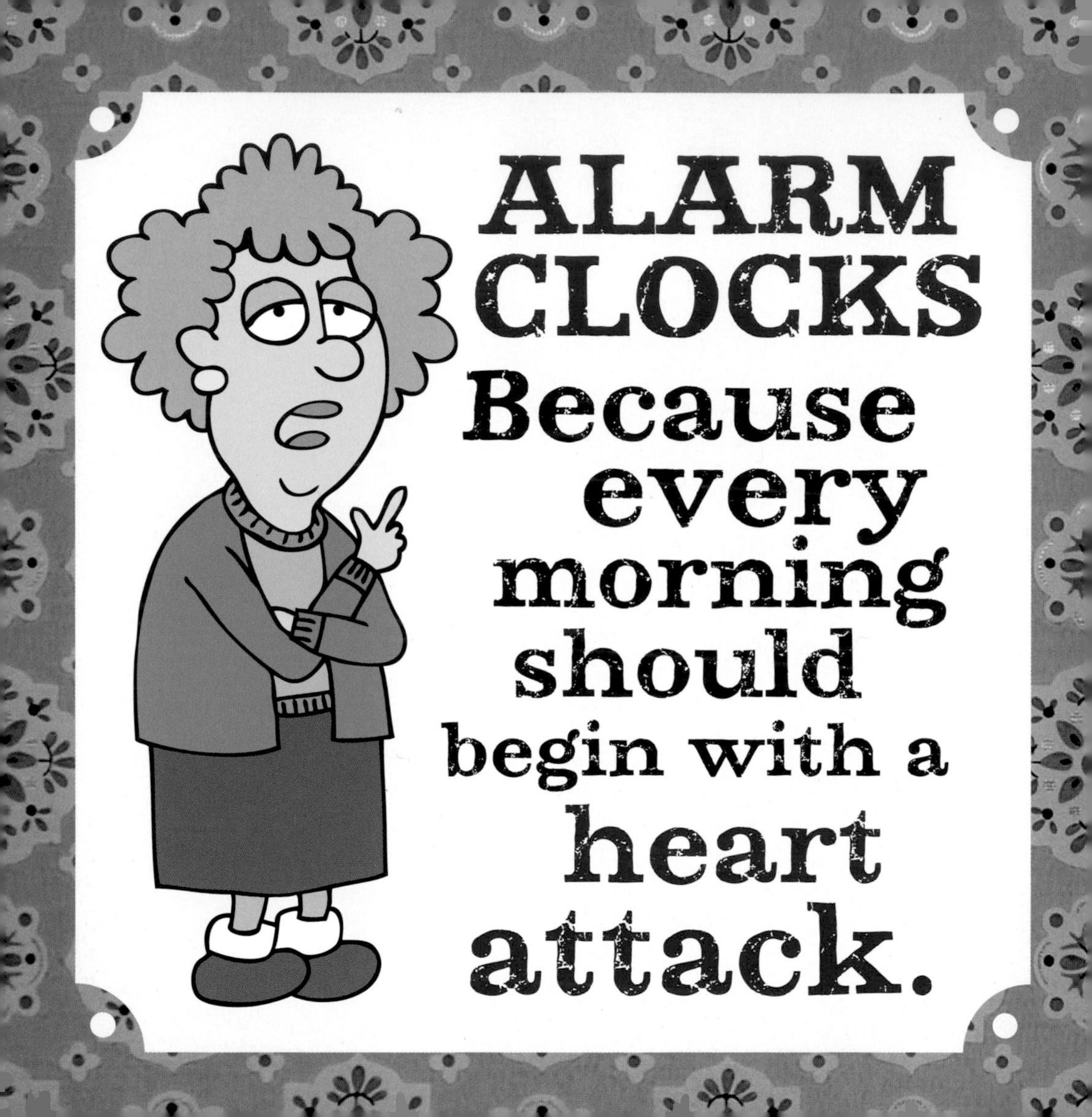
ALARM CLOCKS
Because every morning should begin with a heart attack.

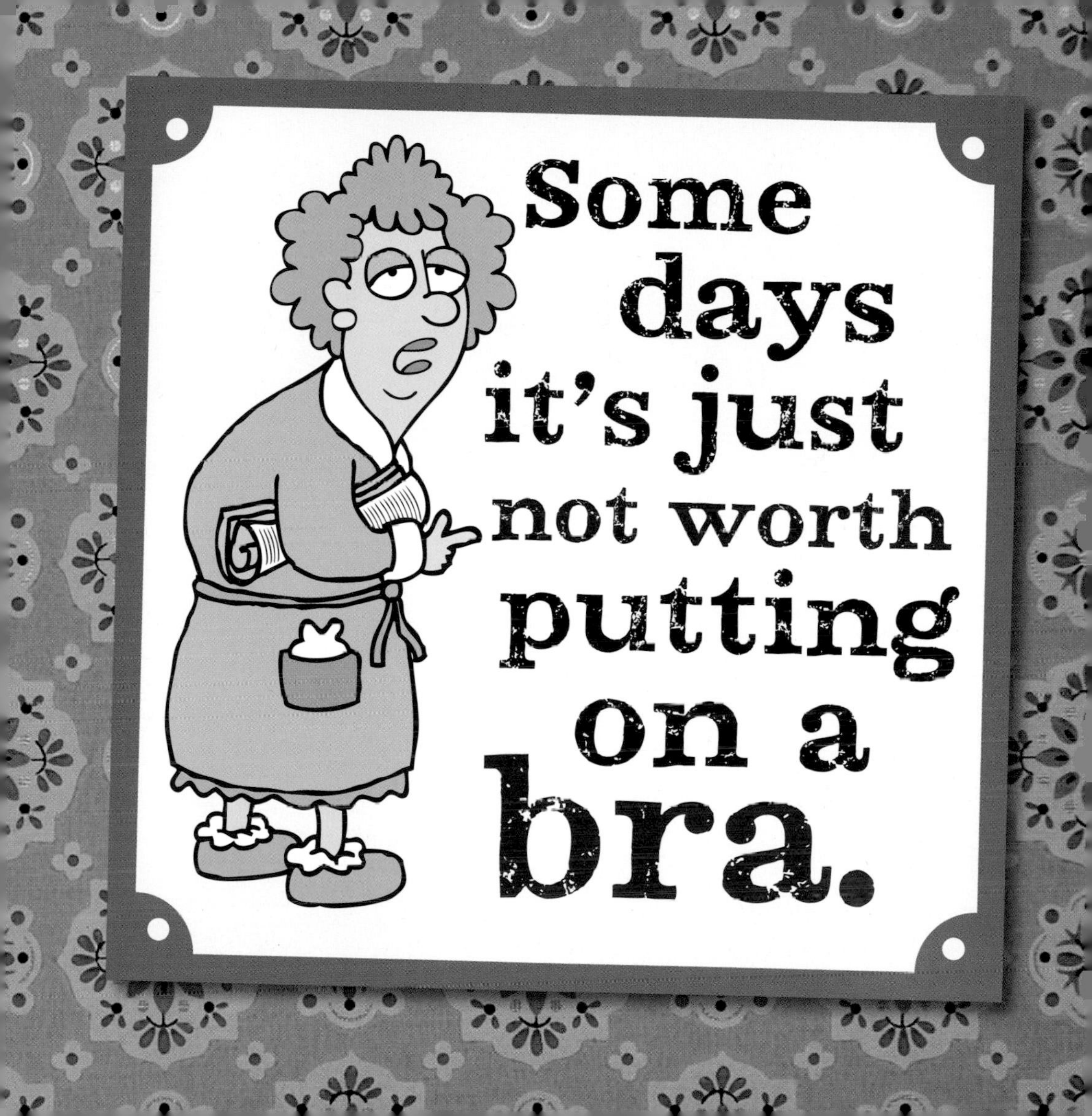
Some days it's just not worth putting on a bra.

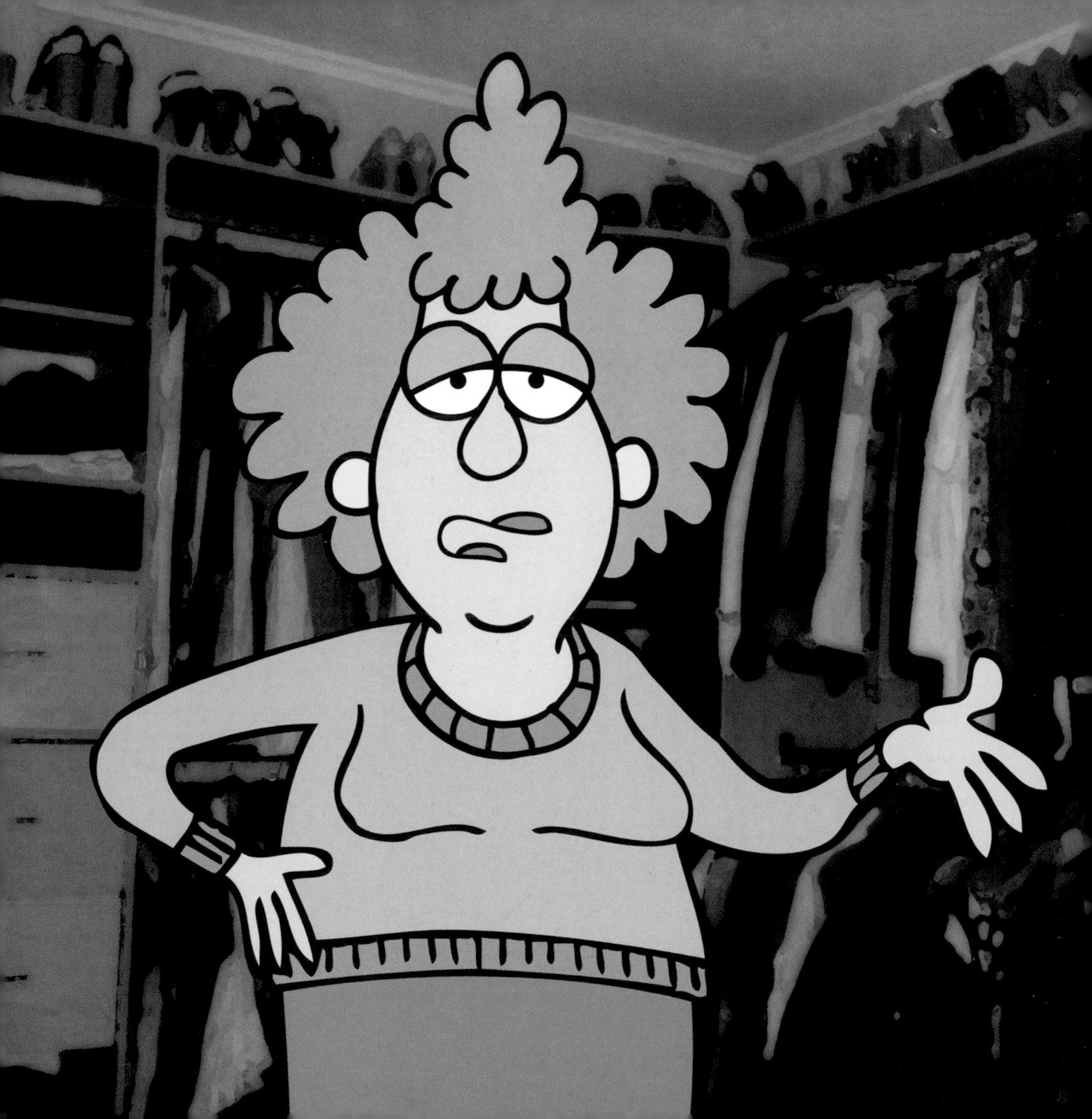

I feel like such a

failure.

I've been shopping for

over 40 years

and I still don't have

anything

to wear.

The good news is—
today, for the first time
in 20 years, I bent down
and touched
my toes.
The
depressing
news is—
I did it
with my
boobs.

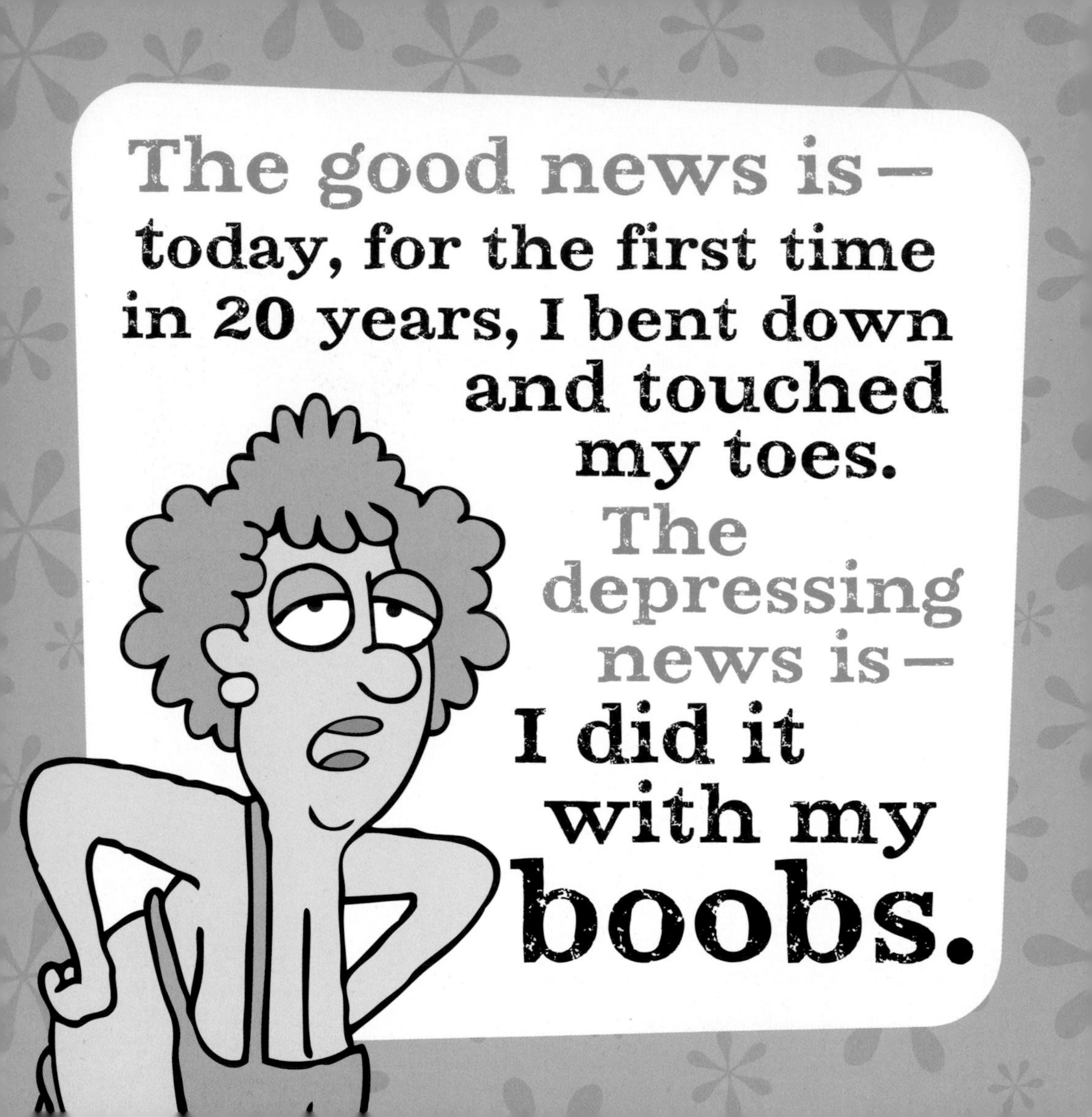

You know your children are growing up when they stop asking you where they came from and refuse to tell you where they're going.

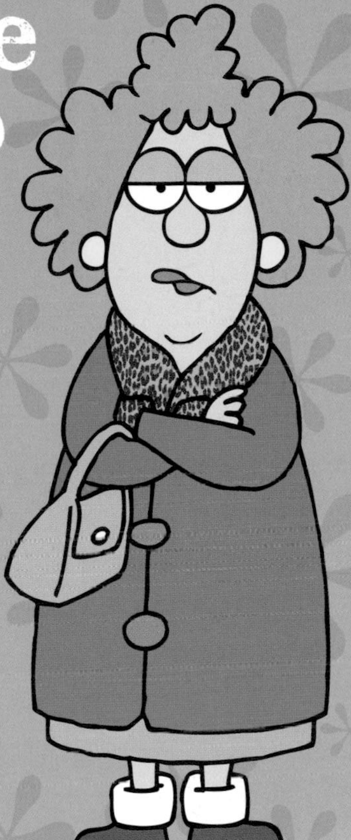

They say there's no fool like an OLD fool—

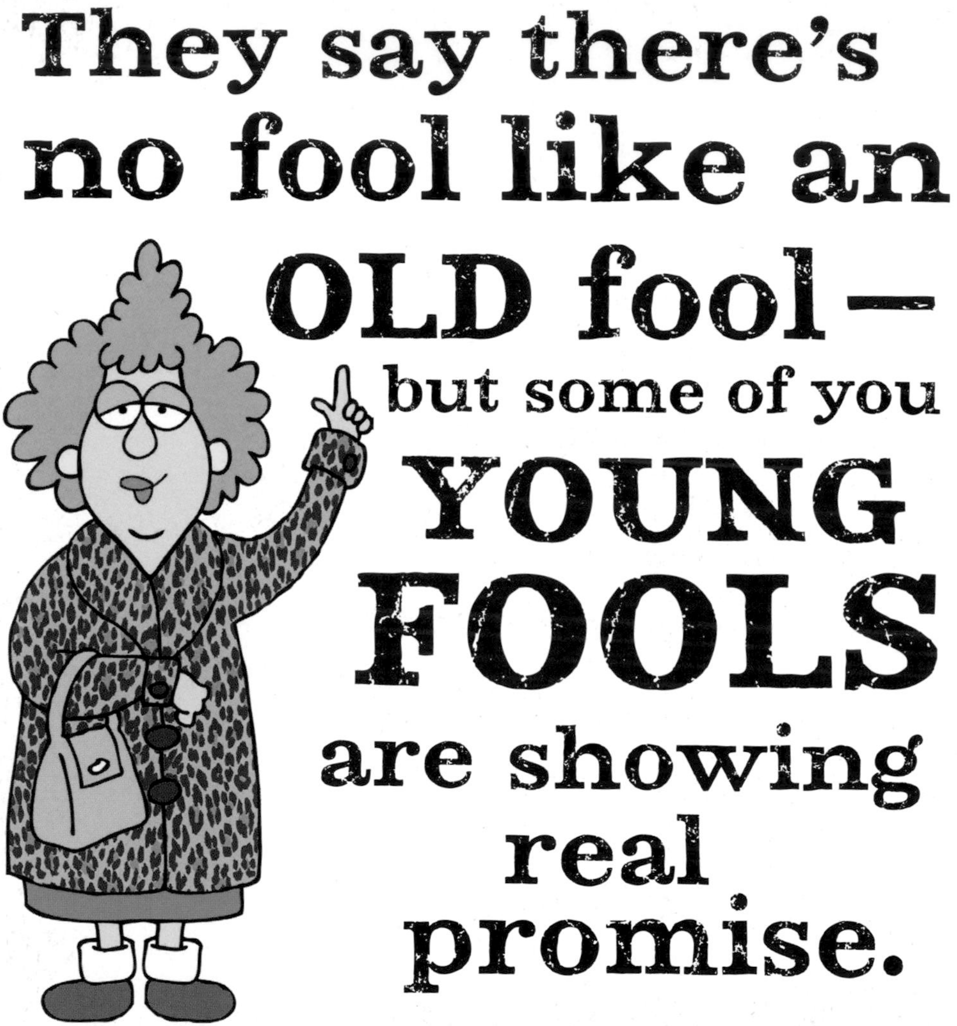

but some of you YOUNG FOOLS are showing real promise.

Getting **OLD** is like being on a **ROLLER COASTER.** There are highs, lows, laughter and tears and, every once in a while, you might just **pee** your pants a little.

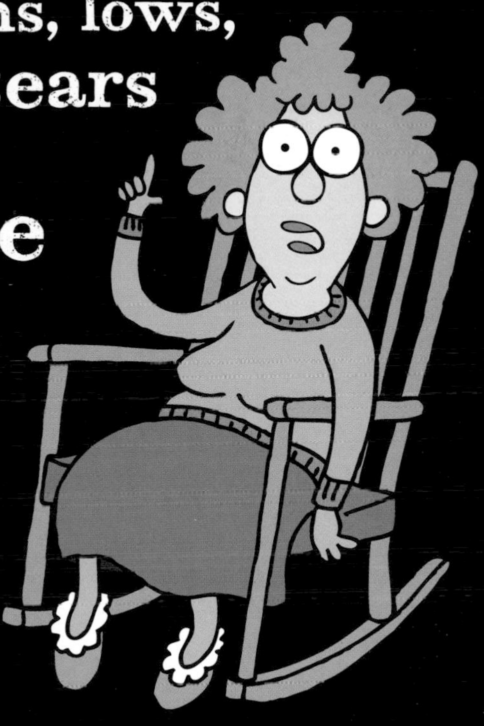

For all the young ladies thinking of getting a **tattoo:** REMEMBER — when you get older, a butterfly on the back becomes a **buzzard in the crack.**

Just because I give you advice doesn't mean I'm **smarter** than you. It just means I've done **more** stupid stuff than you.

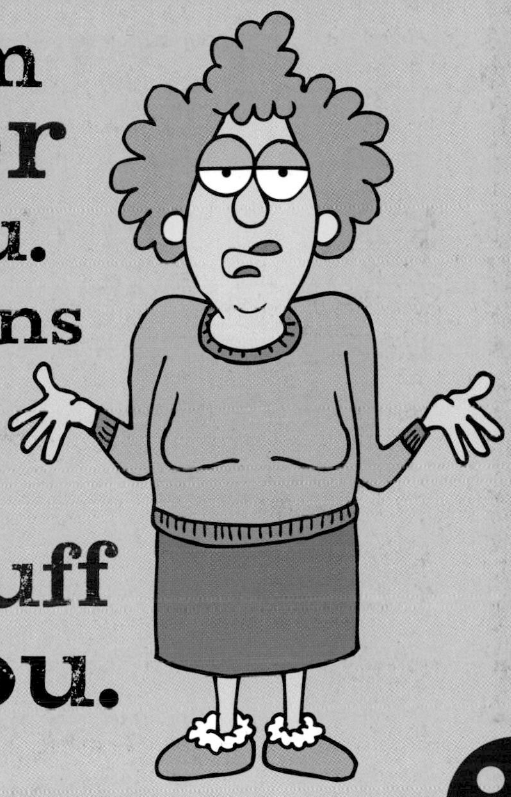

First Edition
17 16 15 14 13   5 4 3 2

Cartoons © 2013 Ged Backland

Published by
Gibbs Smith
P.O. Box 667
Layton, Utah 84041

1.800.835.4993 orders
www.gibbs-smith.com

Illustrations by Dave Iddon @ The Backland Studio
Interiors designed by Dave Iddon
Cover designed by Melissa Dymock
Printed and bound in China

Gibbs Smith books are printed on either recycled, 100% post-consumer
waste, FSC-certified papers or on paper produced from sustainable PEFC-
certified forest/controlled wood source. Learn more at www.pefc.org.

ISBN 13: 978-1-4236-3503-1